AFRICA POLICY
in the Clinton Years
Critical Choices for the
Bush Administration

Significant Issues Series
Timely books presenting current CSIS research and analysis of interest to the
academic, business, government, and policy communities.
Managing editor: Roberta L. Howard

For four decades, the **Center for Strategic and International Studies (CSIS)** has
been dedicated to providing world leaders with strategic insights on—and policy
solutions to—current and emerging global issues.

CSIS is led by John J. Hamre, formerly deputy secretary of defense, who has
been president and CEO since April 2000. It is guided by a board of trustees
chaired by former senator Sam Nunn and consisting of prominent individuals
from both the public and private sectors.

The CSIS staff of 190 researchers and support staff focus primarily on three
subject areas. First, CSIS addresses the full spectrum of new challenges to national
and international security. Second, it maintains resident experts on all of the
world's major geographical regions. Third, it is committed to helping to develop
new methods of governance for the global age; to this end, CSIS has programs on
technology and public policy, international trade and finance, and energy.

Headquartered in Washington, D.C., CSIS is private, bipartisan, and tax-
exempt. CSIS does not take specific policy positions; accordingly, all views
expressed herein should be understood to be solely those of the authors.

The CSIS Press
Center for Strategic and International Studies
1800 K Street, N.W., Washington, D.C. 20006
Telephone: (202) 887-0200   Fax: (202) 775-3199
E-mail: books@csis.org   Web: www.csis.org

AFRICA POLICY
in the Clinton Years
Critical Choices for the Bush Administration

EDITED BY J. STEPHEN MORRISON AND JENNIFER G. COOKE

Foreword by Chester A. Crocker

THE CSIS PRESS

Center for Strategic
and International Studies
Washington, D.C.

Significant Issues Series, Volume 23, Number 4
© 2001 by Center for Strategic and International Studies
Washington, D.C. 20006
Printed on recycled paper in the United States of America
Cover design by Robert L. Wiser, Archetype Press

05   04   03   02   5   4   3

ISSN 0736-7136
ISBN 0-89206-396-3

Library of Congress Cataloging-in-Publication Data
Africa Policy in the Clinton years: critical choices for the Bush administration /
    edited by J. Stephen Morrison and Jennifer G. Cooke; foreword by
    Chester A. Crocker.
        p. cm. — (CSIS significant issues series, ISSN 0736-7136 ; v. 23, no. 4)
    Includes index
    ISBN 0-89206-396-3
        1. Africa—Foreign relations—United States. 2. United States—Foreign
    relations—Africa. 3. United States—Foreign relations—1993–2001.
    I. Morrison, J. Stephen. II. Cooke, Jennifer G. III. Center for Strategic and
    International Studies (Washington, D.C.) IV. Series.
DT38.7.A383 2001
327.7306–dc21   2001005894

CONTENTS

FOREWORD

Chester A. Crocker

WHEN STEVE MORRISON, DIRECTOR OF CSIS'S AFRICA PROGRAM, asked if I would write a foreword for this volume, it occurred to me that things had come full circle. Since my days as Steve's predecessor at CSIS, so many African challenges and crises have come and gone—and in some cases have come back again to demand a place on the U.S. agenda. I wondered if there was much new to be said and whether the chapters of this book, flowing from a series of working groups conducted during 2000, would make compelling reading.

These questions disappeared as soon as I began reading. CSIS's Africa Program has produced a superb collection of policy essays. The experts and scholars mobilized for the project represent some of the best people on these subjects available anywhere in the world. The writing is terse and disciplined. The chapters are concise and readable. The resulting volume represents a veritable guidebook for the conduct of a mainstream, centrist African policy by the U.S. government. Moreover, there is little doubt that these essays have been consulted widely for precisely this reason by people in the Bush administration, the Congress, and the media.

There are several things to be hoped for in a book about America's African policies. The first is realism—and this is a realistic book. The chapters on HIV/AIDS, crisis diplomacy, key bilateral relations, and

CHESTER A. CROCKER is the James R. Schlesinger Professor of Strategic Studies at the Georgetown University School of Foreign Service. During 1977–1980, he was CSIS's director of African Studies.

peace operations and humanitarian response are chilling in their candor about Africa's condition. Take, for example, these words from chapter 5 on relations with Nigeria and South Africa:

> Achieving workable partnerships...will take time, will involve tensions, complex trade-offs, and mutual hesitation, and will not be guaranteed success. Setbacks and frustrations are inevitable. But the reality is that if the United States is to be engaged meaningfully in Africa, it has little choice but to press ahead in testing systematically what is possible....

At times, the realism is hard-hitting and applies directly to the U.S. policymaking arena. Consider this admonition, from chapter 7, on the subject of African humanitarian emergencies: "Conspicuous failure to respond effectively could damage the administration's standing, domestically and internationally, and invite accusations of callousness, ineptitude, and irresponsibility."

Another thing one hopes for in a book about U.S. African policies is balance and a sense of historical perspective. Africa has never figured near the top of the list of U.S. foreign policy priorities. It does not today—and probably never will. The contributors to this volume take due note of the considerable efforts made during the 1990s to draw greater attention to Africa, raise its rhetorical profile in U.S. policy pronouncements, and orchestrate senior-level travel and frequent, visible consultations with African counterparts. Yet, they underscore the reality that the 1990s have been "catastrophic" for Africa, that U.S. actions and responses have often been empty or ineffectual because of reluctance to engage in conflict management and a hollowing out of U.S. diplomatic capabilities in Washington and the field. Major weaknesses, as this book conclusively states, included ineffective coordination with, and attention to, congressional and Allied relationships and a dubious quest for ways to align ourselves with the chimera of "African solutions for African problems" and with a "new generation" of African leaders.

Yet if these chapters make difficult reading for Clinton era officials, they also set the bar very high for their successors in the George W. Bush administration. A number of constructive policy building blocks from the 1990s and earlier are in place and must be sustained—in the areas of trade policy, HIV/AIDS leadership, debt relief, support for reinvigorated security assistance programs, and the strengthening of desperately weak state institutions. A responsible stance toward meeting U.S. obligations to the United Nations is also considered essential: although African national and regional forces can and should be strengthened, for now the United Nations is correctly identified as "the main game in town," all the more so in the wake of the Brahimi report on peacekeeping. U.S. officials are reminded that African policy can do relatively well only if managed through bipartisanship and the sharing of credit as well as burdens.

U.S. officials are urged in these pages to be upfront, candid, and realistic in recognizing the need for tough choices because (as stated in chapter 4) "previous and current resource levels are grossly inadequate for the situations found on the ground." This situation means triage is required, choices are needed, and some priorities must be agreed, especially on intervention questions where the United States must "pick its spots." Officials are urged in specific and well-chosen words to ratchet back the rhetoric of engagement wherever trouble rears its head, to propose action only with the utmost seriousness and in coordination with a Congress that is well informed, closely consulted and thus able to review potential peace operations with equal gravity.

Those readers who are dismayed or disheartened by the "in your face" honesty of these pages may miss the point. The contributors to this collection care passionately and sympathetically about the region and yet are capable of speaking the truth about it. Africa, one can hope, may have had enough of Americans' genuflecting on one altar or another of ideology or political correctness. Contributors understand how much is at stake, how unacceptable it is—politically and morally—for American leaders to backburner this region, and how many U.S. interests (both positive and negative) are influenced by what happens there. Rather than a handbook of disengagement and Afro-pessimism, this volume is a guidebook for realistic and sustainable engagement. Each of the chapters on the African economy and Africa's health crises makes, in its own way, a powerful but carefully argued and nuanced case for U.S. engagement.

To a reader who has participated in the dialogues and debates of scholarly and practitioner Africanists since the late 1960s, it is a pleasure to read this slim volume—both for what it says and for what it avoids. For decades, U.S. policies toward the region have oscillated between poles of engagement and neglect, of romantic embrace and dismissive aloofness, of wide-eyed and one-sided hopefulness and an overwhelming urge to keep African mud off our boots. For decades, U.S. policies toward Africa have been buffeted by a partisanship that caused administrations of one political party to define themselves principally by reversing legacies from their predecessors. At times, leaders in the executive branch and Congress conduct themselves as if they believed that Africa belongs or ought to belong to narrowly based ethnic or religious constituencies.

It is refreshing and reassuring that the contributors to this volume exclude narrow partisanship or any sense that Africa "belongs" to anyone (apart from Africans themselves). The balanced realism—if proposed and sustained by the executive branch, which is the natural place from which to lead in foreign policy—outlined here could build upon existing elements of bipartisan consensus. The road could be cleared for an interest-based and results-oriented set of policies capable of garnering and retaining requisite support from the American polity.

That said, it is fair to ask if people in the Bush administration have read this book and are following its nostrums. Although it remains early to make such an assessment, certain points are fairly clear. First, many of the people who worked in this CSIS project are now managing U.S.-African relations! My sense is that, in the main, they agree today with what they thought last year, which is, to say the least, reassuring. Second, some messages here have clearly been taken to heart—e.g., the need to rebuild, after shocking deterioration, U.S. diplomatic capabilities toward Africa and a clear distancing from the simplistic "good guys versus bad guys" approach to selecting America's partners in the region. The administration's careful and considered approach to picking up the Sudan nettle suggests that a serious effort could be under way to balance domestic politics with the foreign policy merits of the U.S. stance toward that agonized land.

The book's straightforward language in describing the obscenity of Mugabe's self-destructive behavior in Zimbabwe suggests a recognition that he is literally destroying southern Africa's future and that there is no purpose in pretending otherwise. There has been a clear attempt to base policy in some measure on "anchor" states Nigeria and South Africa; and the constraints and limits of that approach also appear to be appreciated.

To be sure, the administration has taken up some of the easier and less challenging policy tasks to date—responding fairly effectively to the HIV/AIDS issues and promoting continued, even expanded, effort on African trade and investment issues. Following the path of least resistance, it has continued to support peace efforts where it inherited a clear and constructive legacy from its predecessors (Ethiopia-Eritrea) and peace operations where there is an element of committed leadership from others (e.g., the British and Nigerians in Sierra Leone). Perhaps the most interesting departure reflecting a careful reading of the lessons in this volume is Washington's recent, determined reopening of diplomatic dialogue on Africa with European allies of the United States—a move that any experienced Africanist understands is a key to effectiveness and traction in the difficult terrain of African conflicts.

Let's hope this collection of essays continues to be at the right hand of U.S. policymakers because they will need it. It is questionable whether Washington can really expect to be effective in Africa if it remains nearly invisible in the Central African/Congo/Great Lakes tangle. This regional complex—not Sudan—is the greatest contemporary challenge to the security and hopes of sub-Saharan Africa, just as Zimbabwe's downward course is the number one threat to the future of southern Africa. As the book says, choices need to be made. Some of them will be made by events on the ground that are simply beyond the reach of U.S. policy. But where U.S. actions, positions, and leadership can make the most difference is where the United States should be focusing its attention. Similarly, the United States can make a difference by not obstructing the constructive leadership efforts of others. Thus, it was a grievously sad hour this past July when American officials went out of their way at the United Nations to obstruct continued, steady movement on the important question of stopping the small arms catastrophe afflicting developing nations, especially those in Africa.

In conclusion, readers of this report are reminded once again of the creative roles think tanks can play in the U.S. system. We can hope that they will continue to do so and keep our eyes on the ball.

ACKNOWLEDGMENTS

"Beyond the Clinton Administration's Africa Policy," the CSIS project that produced this volume, was organized into six working groups, each of which met up to six times between July and December 2000. From the outset, the working group chairs solicited participation from a broad array of senior policymakers, past and present, congressional staff, representatives from academia, the United Nations, nongovernmental organizations, and African and European counterpart institutions. There are thus many contributors to this book, and for their advice on shaping the overall project, the time they were willing to commit, and their thoughtful participation in working group discussions, we are deeply grateful. Participation was excellent across the board, but a few individuals should be singled out for exceptional commitment and outstanding contributions: Helene Gayle, then director of the Center for Disease Control and Prevention's National Center for HIV, STD, and TB Prevention; Todd Summers of Progressive Health Partners; Ambassador Howard Jeter, then deputy assistant secretary at the U.S. State Department's Africa Bureau and now U.S. ambassador to Nigeria; Robert Houdek, director of the National Intelligence Council; Charles Snyder, deputy assistant secretary in the U.S. State Department's Africa Bureau; and Bob Orr, then deputy to the U.S. ambassador to the United Nations and now senior fellow at the CSIS International Security Program.

We thank Lee Hamilton, Mike Van Dusen, and Gilbert Kadiagala of the Woodrow Wilson International Center for Scholars for hosting a conference on December 20, 2000, to vet with a broader audience the study's preliminary findings. We also thank Susan Rice, then U.S. assistant secretary of state for African affairs, and Gayle Smith, then senior director for Africa at the National Security Council, for taking time on two occasions (including the Wilson Center event) to share their insight and offer thoughtful commentary on the near-final working paper drafts.

We are especially grateful to the working group chairs, who, when they first agreed to participate, perhaps did not anticipate just how much we would ask of them. Their sustained effort, intellectual focus, openness to differing viewpoints, and ability to distill group discussions into thoughtful written analysis helped ensure consistent and exceptional participation by working group contributors and are reflected in the quality and balance of the final report.

CSIS wishes to thank the donors whose financial support made the project possible: ExxonMobil, Halliburton Co., Chevron, BP, Citigroup, the Pritzker Foundation, and Texaco. The contents of this volume are, of course, the responsibility of the CSIS Africa Program and do not reflect the views of donor organizations or CSIS as a whole.

Within CSIS, we are most grateful for the support of CSIS president John Hamre; the help and advice of the CSIS Press, including Jim Dunton, Roberta Howard, Donna Spitler, and Maria Farkas; and the CSIS Africa Program interns, particularly Mona Mahboubi and Sarah Lantz, whose help during the summer of 2000 was critical in getting the project up and running. Finally, our heartfelt thanks to Sarah Skorupski, the CSIS Africa Program coordinator, who managed with patience and good humor to keep the many working group sessions on track, and whose ability to juggle many tasks and at the same time attend to countless details has been an invaluable asset to the program.

CHAPTER ONE

PREVIEW OF MAJOR FINDINGS

J. Stephen Morrison and Jennifer G. Cooke

THE YEARS OF BILL CLINTON'S PRESIDENCY SAW unprecedented high-level engagement in Africa and the articulation of a vision of partnership based on consultations and ambitious policy initiatives. The Clinton administration moved to advertise its aims aggressively to the American people and strongly emphasized important new policy paradigms—most conspicuously, global market integration through the Africa Growth and Opportunity Act (AGOA) and investment in security through the Africa Crisis Response Initiative (ACRI). At the same time, private U.S. efforts—the National Summit on Africa and the initiatives of the Corporate Council on Africa—were launched to strengthen a domestic constituency for Africa.

In several areas, substantial results were realized. The United States contributed significantly to the consolidation of the South African, Nigerian, and Mozambican transitions. It systematically enlarged the incorporation of U.S. business perspectives into policy deliberations and, in recognition of rising U.S. energy stakes in Africa, began to formulate new energy policies. Through ACRI it trained an estimated 6,000 peacekeepers. More recently, the Clinton administration mobilized to combat HIV/AIDS and signed into law the AGOA legislation. Arguably, these achievements would not have occurred had not the administration consciously ratcheted up its engagement and investment in Africa.

At the same time, in many policy areas the administration encountered substantial obstacles, linked both to a worsening environment within Africa and to internal administration constraints, that yielded

1

decisions and programmatic initiatives at times themselves invited policy setbacks and controversy, both at home and abroad. This was true, for example, for the late 1993 decision to disengage from Somalia; the April 1994 decision not to mobilize a major international peacekeeping operation against the Rwanda genocide; the decisions in 1997–1998 to ally the United States closely with "new leaders" in Eritrea, Ethiopia, Rwanda, and Uganda; the halting response to the collapse of the Lomé Accord in Sierra Leone; and debate over the administration's approach to the Eritrea-Ethiopia border war. This was true also for the promotion of AGOA and ACRI, each of which stirred unexpected opposition within the United States and Africa.

Against this backdrop, as policy ambitions expanded and became more diversified during the Clinton years, implementation often became unduly complex and difficult to execute and sustain. Frustration and disappointment became most conspicuous in efforts to manage Africa's proliferating crises, now the predominant preoccupation of U.S. and other policymakers.

Disappointing outcomes and skepticism over Africa's future may motivate the current Bush administration, in keeping with its stated inclination to limit U.S. exposure in complex humanitarian crises, to scale back its engagement in Africa significantly. In fact, U.S. national interests call for more, not less, engagement in Africa, and Secretary of State Colin Powell's early public statements and his travel to Africa in May 2001 appeared to confirm that point. The challenge is to define how, where, and to what specific purpose tangible results can be achieved. A policy of continued active engagement in Africa requires a sober, credible approach that spells out U.S. interests, takes account of the lessons of the 1990s, and presents a feasible path forward.

BACKGROUND TO THE CSIS REPORT

In July 2000, the CSIS Africa Program launched, under program director J. Stephen Morrison, a review of U.S. Africa policy. The project aimed to examine major policy initiatives in the Clinton years and evolving challenges in Africa, to summarize and explain policy outcomes, and to advise the new administration on feasible approaches to impending, critical policy decisions in Africa. This final report offers not an encyclopedic review of U.S.-African issues but a series of succinct policy pieces to inform senior policymakers and policy experts on critical priorities and feasible choices.

The project was organized into working groups that address six areas: HIV/AIDS, chaired by J. Stephen Morrison; crisis diplomacy, chaired by Terrence Lyons; peace operations, chaired by Jendayi Frazer and Jeffrey Herbst; critical relations with South Africa and Nigeria, chaired by Princeton Lyman and Gwendolyn Mikell; U.S. economic interests, chaired by Peter Lewis; and humanitarian action, chaired by Victor Tanner and Nan Borton.

Throughout, the project has operated on a nonpartisan, broadly inclusionary basis. The project benefited from the exceptional commitment of its working group chairs and the extensive participation of congressional staff (both Democrat and Republican), senior diplomats and other executive branch officials, representatives of the Bush and Gore presidential campaigns, the corporate sector, nongovernmental groups, and university-based policy experts. In aggregate, 30 working group sessions were held involving more than 115 individuals. Numerous side consultations on specific policies also occurred between July and December.

Initial findings were presented at a December 20, 2000, conference hosted by the Africa Program of the Woodrow Wilson International Center for Scholars, attended by members of the outgoing Clinton administration and advisers to the incoming Bush administration. Comments and suggestions from that conference have been incorporated into the final chapters that follow.

HOW ARE U.S. INTERESTS CHANGING?

Enduring U.S. national interests in Africa, though not strategic, remain highly important. They are grounded in historical linkages between the continent and America's 36 million African Americans. They reside in Africa's supply of more than 15 percent of America's petroleum requirements. And they emanate from U.S. values and goals that continue to be central to global U.S. foreign policy: democracy and respect for human rights; alleviation of human suffering;

strengthening of market economies within an expanding global economic community; and combating the transnational security threats posed by crime, terrorism, money laundering, narcotics trafficking, and global infectious diseases.

These interests inspired the Clinton administration's multiple policy initiatives and the Bush administration's early high-level engagement in Africa. They are also tied to the bipartisan congressional coalitions and diverse interest groups that have endorsed expanded debt relief, new trade and investment policies, heightened support to combat HIV/AIDS, and strengthening of African peacekeeping capacities.

During the Bush administration, U.S. interests in Africa are being reshaped by six dramatic developments.

1. The continent's security, economic vitality, and political coherence are declining—and are at risk of further setbacks.

Africa's economic marginality has worsened—a sizable portion of the continent's citizens survives on less than $1 per day, an inherently unstable reality. Armed intrastate and interstate conflicts have proliferated, several states have failed, and a substantial number of weak states may experience sudden breakdowns. Spillover effects, the armed abrogation of sovereign boundaries, HIV/AIDS, and the regionalization of conflicts impose ever-higher costs.

Hard-won gains in South Africa and Nigeria are at risk if the United States and others do not make the necessary investments in the coming years. There is also today the risk of Africa's further disengagement from the global economy, backlash against the West, and a turn to criminal channels. Debt relief has increasingly become the continental rallying cry to revitalize Africa's viability and win more favorable global trading terms. In comparative global terms, Africa's decline sets it apart conspicuously and presents an urgent, expansive long-term agenda.

2. U.S. bilateral influence and institutional capacities have waned in the aftermath of the Cold War.

U.S. bilateral influence has dropped, even while Africa's profile in U.S. foreign policy has been elevated in recent years. Diplomatic capacities in Washington and key U.S. embassies have been hollowed out, and material resources have diminished. In combination, these realities force us to confront the central question: how are we to bridge the gap between means and ends and overcome mounting skepticism that U.S. national interests can be effectively advanced in Africa?

3. The HIV/AIDS pandemic places Africa in a new global context and is inexorably reshaping U.S. foreign policy stakes in Africa and beyond.

In coming years, the global HIV/AIDS pandemic will dominate U.S. foreign policy interests in Africa and test U.S. leadership in multiple ways. It will demand new forms of diplomacy, new concerted action between Congress and the executive branch, new budgetary commitments, and new innovative programs. It will make orphans a high humanitarian priority, draw increasing attention to the human rights of persons living with HIV, highlight the empowerment of women, and alter approaches to economic growth, internal state viability, and transnational security threats. Creating and strengthening elementary health infrastructures will become an essential prerequisite both to carrying out effective programs and to conducting effective diplomacy.

HIV/AIDS will require grappling with emerging ethical and public health risks that grow out of the misapplication of medications, emergence of new resistant viral strains, and toxic reactions to medications. It will also often force very tough moral choices. The United States will be asked to ration finite resources among competing, urgent requirements to reduce extreme suffering and prolong life. It will also be under pressure to define credible, realistic time frames and measures of effectiveness in the midst of considerable uncertainty.

A profound shift in U.S. foreign policy is already under way in dealings with southern and eastern Africa—epicenter of the pandemic and home to 26 million of the world's 36 million persons infected by HIV, where more than 17 million persons have already died and 11 million children have been orphaned. In 2001, the urgency surrounding the pandemic has become increasingly palpable, while the overall context has evolved swiftly. The sudden drop in commercial pricing of anti-retroviral medications, and the anticipation that a similar drop may occur for palliative medications, have radically altered the landscape with respect to cost, international political momentum, and the attention paid to pharmaceuticals versus prevention and other urgent priorities.

4. The increasingly important U.S. energy stakes in Africa will in coming years reach near-strategic proportions.

More than 15 percent of America's oil now comes from Central and West Africa. In the coming years this non-Gulf source of oil will exceed 20 percent and U.S. investment in the energy sector will more than double. These trends will tie U.S. interests ever more tightly to Angola, Nigeria, Chad, and Equatorial Guinea—unsteady states with weak institutions and a legacy of corruption and internal conflict. In the case of Angola and Nigeria, military and political leadership will also continue to play a crucial security role in their respective regions. The $3.7 billion Chad-Cameroon pipeline, whose construction was just launched, is the continent's largest infrastructure project and will command significant future international scrutiny. This precedent-setting experiment links the interests of energy corporations, the World Bank, participant governments, and nongovernmental bodies and seeks to channel revenues to verifiable developmental ends.

5. Recent genocide, war crimes, and other atrocities—and the threat of recurrent episodes—are placing U.S. policy interests in Africa in a new global context.

The legacy of U.S. inaction in the face of the 1994 Rwanda genocide now combines with controversy surrounding U.S. policy toward the Revolutionary United Front (RUF) in Sierra Leone, mounting allegations of genocide and war crimes in Sudan and violations of humanitarian law in Angola, and awareness that atrocities could recur suddenly in Burundi, eastern Congo, and West Africa.

How to respond preemptively and effectively to this threat remains complex and highly problematic. But to ignore or underestimate the threat, until it is too late to do anything meaningful, is to put at serious risk the next administration's standing—among the American people, in Africa, and among the worldwide community now mobilized around issues of genocide and ending impunity.

6. The modality and structure of international terrorism are shifting.

Terrorist groups beginning in the 1990s have operated within more nebulous and loosely organized structures than in previous decades, as motivations shifted from narrow political goals to broader ideological and anti-Western impulses. To accomplish their goals, terrorist groups increasingly require free movement through countries and critical transit points worldwide, and terrorist activity is most likely to thrive in those places where borders are porous, security lax, and state capacities weak. For these reasons, African states are particularly at risk of becoming terrorist hubs or havens. The August 1998 bombings of the U.S. embassies in Nairobi and Dar es Salaam, which killed 12 U.S. citizens, 245 Kenyans and Tanzanians, and injured thousands, brought this fact starkly home and underlined the emergent need for U.S.-African cooperation in rooting out terrorist activity and eliminating the conditions that allow it to thrive.

FINDINGS AND RECOMMENDATIONS

In chapter 2, Stephen Morrison examines U.S. policy toward the HIV/AIDS pandemic, which threatens to overwhelm already weak state capacities and undermine the economic and political stability of many African states. He advises the Bush administration to build on a growing international consensus to do more, on an urgent basis, to enlarge critical programmatic interventions known to achieve results. It should concentrate on creating elementary health infrastructure in Africa and ensure coherent high-level leadership in Washington, the definition of long-term policy goals and a rise of U.S. resource commitments to more than $1 billion by 2002. The United States should systematically strengthen its internal organizational capacity and forge collaborative partnerships with other international organizations and leaders to support the new global trust fund and the activities of UNAIDS, the joint United Nations (UN) program on HIV/AIDS. The administration will need to work in concert with the G-8, World Trade Organization (WTO), World Health Organization (WHO), and UN to refine international trade rules on key drugs and tackle the difficult controversies that will persist over competing priorities. While accelerating and enlarging education, prevention, and care activities that have been proven effective, the United States must also enhance its understanding of the relationship between AIDS, development, and security.

Chapter 3 examines U.S. diplomatic efforts to prevent or resolve African conflicts. Terrence Lyons advises the Bush administration to take an intensive high-level leadership role in only a few select conflicts where opportunities exist and stakes are high. Implementation of the Ethiopia-Eritrea peace accord, support for a peace process in Sierra Leone, and proactive leadership to head off potential crises in Zimbabwe deserve priority consideration. But high-level engagement in select conflicts should not lead the administration to turn its back on other conflicted areas or ignore the need for crisis prevention. In situations where peace processes are moribund or floundering, the United States should engage broadly, in collaboration with European and African allies, remaining vigilant for opportunities for action and leadership. As of this writing, Sudan and the Democratic Republic of Congo fall into this category, but there are signs that opportunities for heightened U.S. engagement are emerging. To pursue an effective diplomatic policy requires substantial investments in human resources within the Department of State's Africa bureau and in U.S. embassies in Africa.

How the United States responds to Africa's wars will profoundly affect the entirety of U.S. policy toward Africa. In chapter 4 Jendayi Frazer and Jeffrey Herbst examine U.S. investments in security operations to end Africa's proliferating conflicts. They argue that the United States should exercise leadership with allies where immediate progress is possible and essential—most notably, in West Africa, in support of the Algiers Ethiopia-Eritrea peace settlement and, as circumstances warrant, in Congo. The United States should be highly selective in choosing when and where it will intervene to commit actual security assistance, concentrating its resources on a few "spots" in ways that strengthen African and UN capacities. The Bush administration is urged to reorganize its programs to make them more coherent and better articulate its policy and goals to Congress.

In chapter 5, Princeton Lyman and Gwendolyn Mikell call on the administration to strengthen bilateral relations with South Africa and Nigeria—two countries whose stability is essential to the future viability of the continent and with whom coherent, reliable partnerships are necessary for effective U.S. policy in Africa. In South Africa, the United States should define a high-level mechanism of engagement to succeed the Binational Commission established by the Clinton administration. South Africa's economy remains fragile, and the United States should focus on stimulating economic growth and expanding assistance to support critical infrastructure. The Bush administration should engage the South African leadership on collaborative responses to the growing crisis in Zimbabwe and to the HIV/AIDS pandemic. In Nigeria, the United States should work to buttress a still fragile democratic transition. The administration must, as a first priority, restore U.S. diplomatic capacities in Nigeria and seek to sustain a high-level bilateral dialogue that includes debt relief, resource distribution, and corruption, as well as consultations on how best to support Nigeria's peacekeeping role within ECOMOG and the United Nations. The United States should also begin early on to enlarge contacts across the political spectrum and prepare for Nigeria's next elections.

In chapter 6, Peter Lewis examines the pursuit of U.S. economic interests in Africa, including rising energy stakes, trade and investment, debt relief, and development assistance. With U.S. energy stakes expected to rise to near-strategic in the next decade, the Bush administration should articulate and fund a coherent energy policy and more effectively engage the private sector and European allies to cooperate on policy goals, including human rights, environmental protection, and governance reforms. Although trade and investment between Africa and the United States have been the subject of much recent legislation, Africa remains marginalized within the global economy. The United States should work to promote trade and investment in Africa by building on the African Growth and Opportunity Act passed by Congress in 2000 and expanding complementary efforts—by the Overseas Private Investment Corporation, the Export-Import Bank, and the Office of the U.S. Trade Representative, among others—that were initiated in the Clinton administration. At the same time, the new administration should exercise leadership, at home and abroad, on debt reduction for Africa and support faster and deeper debt relief through broadening and simplifying the eligibility requirements contained in the multilateral HIPC (Heavily Indebted Poor Countries) initiative. Finally, the administration should restore appropriate assistance levels, coordinate assistance more effectively with a broader strategy for Africa, and incorporate the U.S. Agency for International Development (USAID) more fully into the policy process. Aid effectiveness could be further enhanced through selective partnerships with countries most likely to pursue essential reforms.

The final chapter, by Victor Tanner and Nan Borton, addresses how the Bush administration should strengthen U.S. government humanitarian action in Africa. The next four years will see persistent humanitarian challenges in Africa—many tied to the continent's violent conflicts, others to drought and the HIV/AIDS pandemic. Domestic pressure for the administration to respond rapidly and visibly will also persist, and there is growing recognition within the government and senior foreign policy circles that U.S. emergency assistance needs to be systematically strengthened. The moral and strategic case for engagement must be effectively communicated to Congress and the U.S. public. Programmatic attention to human rights, protection of civilian populations, internally displaced persons, and the rule of law should be strengthened, as should the leadership and coherence of U.S humanitarian programs to avoid redundancy and increase accountability. The United States must clarify its strategies in critical crisis zones such as Sudan, eastern Congo, and Zimbabwe and take concrete steps toward mitigating the unintended negative consequences of relief.

AN EMERGENT APPROACH

Several priority advisories emerge across the six working groups. In combination, they outline an approach for high-level U.S. engagement in Africa.

- *Be realistic, tough-minded, and candid about U.S. interests and capacities, expectations of partners, and benchmarks for progress.*

Prospects for quick, high returns are low. Odds of embarrassing near-term setbacks are high. Achievable benchmarks should be laid out overtly. Progress should be measured over the medium and long term and openly sold as such. U.S. credibility is not enhanced—indeed it is damaged—by striking a pose at high levels with inadequate follow-up. Rhetoric needs to be carefully aligned with commitments of political will and resources. Under-resourced initiatives should not be pursued.

- *Be selective, set priorities, consolidate efforts.*

Top priorities should include HIV/AIDS; concentrating crisis diplomacy on Sierra Leone, Zimbabwe, and advancement of the Ethiopia-Eritrea Algiers Accord; and strengthening relations with South Africa and Nigeria, the two largest and most influential African democracies, with the greatest influence within their region and as representatives of the African viewpoint in international fora.

Other important goals should include building adequate readiness and quick response when opportunities to promote peace or threats of genocide appear in chronic crisis areas, such as Congo and Burundi; expanding debt relief; deepening trade and investment opportunities; elaborating a coherent U.S. energy policy; and supporting bilateral and international efforts to end impunity and build the rule of law.

- *Rebuild U.S. diplomatic capacities and better organize the administration's internal workings.*

U.S. diplomatic capacities in Washington and in key embassies in Africa have declined, far more than in any other region of the world. To be effective, these capacities must be guaranteed and, where deficient, systematically restored—in both Washington and U.S. embassies, especially in Abuja, Pretoria, Harare, Khartoum, Abidjan, Kinshasa, Addis Ababa, Asmara, and Nairobi. This goal can only be achieved through exceptional efforts. It is essential to clarify U.S. policy goals and ensure institutional coherence and leadership in key policy areas across agencies, including USAID, which often has a tenuous link to

U.S. foreign policy goals. Peace operations, HIV/AIDS, and humanitarian action are policy areas where considerable progress can be realized if there is a concerted high-level effort to better focus the internal workings and available resources of the next administration.

■ *Forge a robust compact with Congress.*

The United States cannot achieve meaningful results on the cheap. Indeed, under-resourced initiatives frequently backfire. If congressional support is not nurtured aggressively on a sustained basis—at the leadership level—the next administration will not be in a position to cover the gap between ambitions and resources. A promising congressional bipartisan consensus exists in key issue areas: HIV/AIDS, trade and investment, debt relief, selective support to UN peacekeeping, and strengthening of African peacekeeping capacities. The next administration should, and can, build from that base to win increased resource commitments in these select priority areas.

■ *Build strategic collaboration with European allies, select African states, and the United Nations.*

New, dynamic international coalitions will be essential to an effective U.S. policy—and not easy to erect. Transatlantic alliances withered in the 1990s, during a period when the individual bilateral influence of major Western powers declined. European policies toward Africa, on peacekeeping and economic assistance, have been shifting in a manner that improves the potential for cooperation with the United States, but these synergies have not been fully exploited.

Together with its allies the United States needs to forge coalitions with key African states that affect priority conflicts and the economic future of the continent as a whole. It will be critical to move beyond mutual wariness and halting diplomatic and security cooperation with South Africa and Nigeria and reaffirm the centrality of the United Nations to restoring security, battling HIV/AIDS, and achieving effective humanitarian action.

CHAPTER TWO

U.S. POLICY TOWARD HIV/AIDS IN AFRICA

MOMENTUM, OPPORTUNITIES, AND URGENT CHOICES

J. Stephen Morrison

DURING THE BUSH ADMINISTRATION, the epic HIV/AIDS tragedy now swiftly unfolding will reshape Africa and inexorably dominate U.S. foreign policy toward the continent. Africa today stands at the epicenter of the HIV/AIDS pandemic. Of the world's 25 most AIDS-affected countries, 24 are African. Of the 36.1 million children and adults living with HIV/AIDS worldwide, 25.3 million are Africans. Of the 21.8 million people who have died from HIV/AIDS, 80 percent are Africans.

HIV/AIDS gravely compromises Africa's economic promise, social stability, and security, and that threat is expected to worsen in coming years. To varying degrees, the pandemic will heavily strain the acutely affected states in Africa, many of which are already weak, and generate new forms of instability. Its impact will be felt in militaries, policing, teaching and health professions, economic viability and food security, the emergence of huge orphan populations, national leaders' legitimacy, and democratic governance. Some African states will suffer a significant erosion of capacity, and there is a high probability that some states will fail. Other states like Uganda and Senegal, if able to sustain their prevention and care programs, will manage the destabilizing potential of HIV/AIDS reasonably well.

HIV/AIDS will trigger changes in U.S. diplomacy, command a significant proportion of future U.S. foreign assistance, make orphans a high humanitarian priority, draw increasing attention to the human rights of persons living with HIV and to the empowerment of women, and alter approaches to economic growth, internal state viability, and transnational security threats. Creating and strengthening elementary health infrastructures will become an essential prerequisite both to carrying out effective programs and to conducting effective diplomacy.

HIV/AIDS will test U.S. leadership in multiple ways. It will demand new forms of diplomatic engagement in Africa, new concerted action between Congress and the executive branch, new budgetary commitments, and new innovative programs. It will require grappling with emergent ethical and public health risks that grow out of the misapplication of medications, emergence of new resistant viral strains, and toxic reactions to medications. It will also force very tough moral choices, as resources are rationed among competing, urgent requirements to reduce extreme suffering and prolong life. There will also be rising pressure to define credible, realistic time frames and measures of effectiveness, in the midst of considerable uncertainty.

In 2000 and early 2001, the urgency surrounding the pandemic became increasingly palpable, as the overall context evolved swiftly. The sudden drop in early 2001 in commercial pricing of antiretroviral medications, and the anticipation that a similar drop may occur for palliative medications, radically altered the landscape with respect to cost, international political momentum, and the attention paid to pharmaceuticals versus prevention and other urgent priorities. Through actions by UN secretary general Kofi Annan, Nigerian president Olusegun Obasanjo, U.S. president George W. Bush, and others, there was significant sudden movement toward the establishment of a global trust fund, in the lead up to the June 2001 UN General Assembly Special Session on HIV/AIDS and the G-8 summit in Genoa.

The Bush administration entered power at a promising moment to shape the global approach to HIV/AIDS, centered upon Africa. Despite many uncertainties, there is at present a surprising level of hope and opportunity. At its core is a new international consensus— spurred by an emergent bipartisan congressional coalition, key African leaders (e.g., former president Nelson Mandela, and current presidents Festus Mogae, Olusegun Obasanjo, and Yoweri Museveni), White House activism, the UN General Assembly, UNAIDS, the World Bank, the G-8, heightened media interest, and expanding corporate initiatives. Its shared objective is to do more, on an urgent basis, to carry forward essential multisectoral interventions, in partnership with African governmental and nongovernmental bodies, which increasingly have been shown to bring concrete results. A few countries in Africa are now showing stable or reduced infection rates. Overall, the estimate for new HIV infections in Africa was 3.8 million for 2000, compared with 4 million in 1999.

Early in its tenure, the Bush administration can seize on the current momentum to lay out clear policy goals and expected concrete outcomes by

- strengthening the administration's internal coordination capacity;

- securing substantial new funds to fight HIV/AIDS in Africa, reaching a level of at least $1.5 billion in the first two years of the administration, concentrated on accelerating and enlarging essential activities;

- launching high-level initiatives to spur other donors to commit more to fight HIV/AIDS and ensure that emergent global mechanisms are well governed and swift in delivery;

- strengthening the U.S. grasp of the disease's impact on development and security; and

- refining international trade rules that influence access to HIV-related drugs.

U.S. leadership is pivotal. If the United States chooses to lead robustly, it will be able to claim credit for breaking new ground in defining and implementing the agenda for a critical global issue, even if some individual initiatives founder and new hard lessons are learned. Although the United States should not, and will not, carry full responsibility for the international community's response, its leadership and increased contribution will be essential—to demonstrate American resolve, drive ground-level partnerships forward, and leverage other bilateral and multilateral contributions.

If the United States chooses not to respond robustly, the window of opportunity that exists today may close, generating enduring recriminations, ineffectual half-measures, and disarray in building the basis for an effective global approach to the HIV/AIDS pandemic. Although it is not certain that quickening action by the international community and African counterparts can stanch the advance of HIV/AIDS in the most heavily impacted areas, what is certain, based on the experiences of the 1990s, is that a weak, ad hoc, and late international response today will contribute to unparalleled human suffering, economic decline, and political upheaval in the next decade.

At the end of the 1990s, the United States began to fully recognize that HIV/AIDS is not simply another in a string of crises on a crisis-prone continent. It is a colossus that, in a large segment of Africa, raced far in front of most African leaders, who were in denial, as well as donors and international organizations, who were complacent or disinterested. The central question now is how to establish effective partnerships within Africa that, operating on the basis of the new international consensus, effectively decrease infection rates and provide access to care for the millions living with AIDS.

Any future strategy of heightened engagement will benefit considerably from the emergent multisectoral doctrine—derived from experiences in Uganda, Thailand, Senegal, and elsewhere—of what is required to reverse infection rates, begin to provide access to care and treatment services, and advance applied research on vaccines and other medical technologies. That doctrine's starting point is the forging of new, effective partnerships in Africa: with committed African leaders who mobilize relevant ministries, social sectors, church bodies, and media—to raise awareness, mobilize national resources, and reduce the social stigma attached to the disease. A core preventive goal is to achieve concrete behavioral change through early aggressive interventions among populations likely to contract and spread HIV. A closely related goal is incorporating people living with HIV/AIDS into deliberations and the full range of programs. Priority programs include condom distribution, treatment of sexually transmitted diseases, expanded mother-to-child transmission prevention programs, care for orphans, civic awareness campaigns, and systematic integration of community organizations. Voluntary counseling and treatment are increasingly emphasized for prevention, linked with expanded access to cost-effective drugs for palliative care and the treatment of related or opportunistic diseases—most critically tuberculosis.

The outcomes of programmatic interventions in the next few years will heavily affect Africa's future and important U.S. interests in mitigating Africa's proliferating crises, promoting its integration into the global economy, and ensuring reliable access to increasingly important sources of energy. Outcomes will also set powerful precedents for how the United States copes with global infectious diseases.

In effect, Africa provides the prelude to future HIV/AIDS-related developments in Asia, the Caribbean, Central and South America, and countries of the former Soviet Union, where the pandemic has already begun to have a major impact. How the United States engages on HIV/AIDS in Africa will inevitably shape the future U.S. response in other parts of the world. For these reasons, U.S. national interests in combating HIV/AIDS in Africa—on moral, humanitarian, economic, and transnational security grounds—will increasingly be understood in global terms. HIV/AIDS will alter American perceptions of Africa, how the United States addresses Africa's multiple, proliferating crises, and the position Africa assumes in U.S. global interests.

THE SCOPE AND NATURE OF THE PANDEMIC IN AFRICA

HIV/AIDS threatens a wide reversal of development gains achieved in the past several decades and could create new transnational security threats. Of the more than 21 million people who have died thus far from AIDS worldwide, more than 17 million are Africans. This pattern will persist for the foreseeable future, only on a vaster scale. In the next decade alone AIDS is projected to leave up to one-quarter of the citizens of the most acutely affected African countries dead, orphan 27 million children, reduce already marginalized economies by 20 percent, and severely strain fragile, or already failing, health and other government structures.

As mortality rates skyrocket, life expectancy in many African countries will drop from more than 60 years to less than 40 years (indeed, in several countries this has already happened). HIV prevalence now exceeds 10 percent of adults between the ages of 15 and 49 in the 16 African countries where HIV/AIDS has taken its firmest hold. The continental average is now 8.6 percent as opposed to 1.1 percent worldwide. HIV/AIDS in Africa is spread overwhelmingly through heterosexual contact. It infects women, especially young girls, disproportionately, and has begun to enfeeble critical social assets, such as educators and health professionals. It increasingly consumes the meager public health budgets of those countries hardest hit. Today, it has moved to the fore the tough question of how much, and from which competing budgetary demands (e.g., the military), Africa's leaders will reallocate scarce resources to HIV/AIDS.

The Bush administration should assume that during its tenure prevalence rates among adults could rise swiftly in several additional key African countries. Prevalence of HIV infections among South African adults went from 1 percent in 1990 to just under 20 percent in 2000. In the past eight years, Botswana's infections increased threefold to 38.5 percent of the adult population. For several other countries where HIV prevalence is rising, such as Nigeria, Ethiopia, Ghana, Angola, and Namibia, similar figures are quite probable in the next few years.

Africa's essential quandary is that deep poverty both helps spread HIV/AIDS and deters quick action. Without minimal effective health infrastructure to provide information, education, testing, counseling, and care, few can grasp the connection between behavior and illness, few know they are ill, and few who are infected can find the means to prolong their lives and minimize their suffering. Poverty and poor health care contribute to the high prevalence of sexually transmitted diseases, which accelerates the spread of HIV, as well as tuberculosis and other infectious diseases that hasten death among those ill with AIDS.

THE AWAKENING

The year 1999 marked a turning point in U.S. policy toward the global HIV/AIDS pandemic. Into early 1998, the U.S. government's resources dedicated to HIV/AIDS in Africa, as well as the resources committed by other major powers, had plateaued. The most dramatic evidence of this was when AIDS scarcely surfaced as a focal concern during President Clinton's March 1998 12-day trip to Africa. The United States in the late 1990s spent approximately $10 billion a year for the 800,000 HIV-infected persons in the United States, including vaccine research. In this same period its overseas commitments toward the other 30 million infected persons, of whom 70 percent are African, stayed at an annual level of $130 million to $140 million (of which approximately 60 percent went to Africa).

Beginning in the latter half of 1998 and accelerating in 1999, donor disinterest, matched by denial among the majority of African leaders, gave way to a surge of activism in both Congress and the administration. This changed U.S. trade policies and elevated U.S. rhetorical and financial commitments to battling HIV/AIDS overseas.

In 1999, the administration launched an initiative, Leadership and Investment in Fighting an Epidemic (LIFE), that added $100 million to global HIV/AIDS programs, concentrating on 14 African countries and India. In January 2000, before the UN Security Council—the first ever Security Council special session to focus on a health-related issue—the administration argued that the AIDS pandemic reached well beyond a health crisis and now constituted a threat to global security, the viability of states, and economic development. On that occasion, the administration called for an additional $100 million for HIV/AIDS education and prevention with heavy emphasis on Africa. Shortly thereafter, in his February 2000 address to the National Summit on Africa, President Clinton appealed to African leaders and citizens to deal more openly with the HIV/AIDS crisis and pledged greater U.S. efforts. He repeated similar themes during his August 2000 visit to Nigeria.

In May 2000 President Clinton announced, in an executive order, that he would not allow U.S. government agencies to impose penalties or sanctions on African countries facing medical emergencies for pursuing (1) "parallel imports" (purchasing patented pharmaceuticals from an inexpensive source in a third country) or (2) "compulsory licensing" (commissioning a domestic firm to produce a medication after forcing negotiated terms with the patent holder), so long as they were not in formal violation of the World Trade Organization's international property rights agreement. Just prior to the July AIDS2000 conference in Durban, South Africa, the Ex-Im Bank announced a $1 billion export purchase guarantee to facilitate acquisition of AIDS medications and related requirements.

In fiscal year 2000, $168 million of a global total of $235 million was pledged to Africa. In fiscal year 2001, global commitments by the United States toward HIV/AIDS amount to $464.5 million; that includes a $125-million increase in USAID's HIV/AIDS programs, and a tripling of the Center for Disease Control's (CDC) global HIV/AIDS programs (from $35 million to $106.5 million). Roughly half of the $464.5 million is allocated to Africa.

In this same period, Congress played an ever-larger—and critically important—role. Through a series of hearings and emergency ad hoc measures, it passed enlarged assistance packages that had begun to attract new forms of bipartisan support, including authorization to create a two-year, $300-million World Bank Trust Fund.

In retrospect, circumstances had reached a tipping point in 1999–2000, creating a sense of urgency within the administration and Congress to commit higher resources and energy to combating Africa's HIV/AIDS crisis. Several administration initiatives in the late 1990s—on trade and investment, debt relief, and peacekeeping training—had raised the overall profile of Africa in U.S. foreign policy. Equally critical were repeated high-level visits to Africa in 1998–1999 by the staff of the White House AIDS Policy Office, numerous cabinet and subcabinet officers, and several congressional delegations.

Other vital factors also prompted the administration, Congress, and G-8 member states to move beyond business as usual. In the late 1990s, new data compiled by the Joint United Nations Program on HIV/AIDS (UNAIDS), and reinforced by multiple other sources, starkly conveyed the enormity and complexity of the HIV/AIDS crisis and put a special focus on orphans. Over the course of the decade, the determined analytical, advocacy, and organizational work of the U.S. Agency for International Development, the Centers for Disease Control and Prevention, the National Institutes of Health, the Census Bureau, the UN, the World Bank, and other national ministries had reached a critical mass. Their actions elevated and sustained the profile of HIV/AIDS in Africa before senior policymakers, encouraged enhanced in-depth coverage by the major media, and prompted domestic polls that revealed support among the American people for expanded international HIV/AIDS programs. Perhaps most important, they consolidated an emergent international consensus on the essential elements of a multisectoral approach to combat HIV/AIDS.

RISING OPPORTUNITIES, RISING HAZARDS

The lag period of the 1990s has ended, and the United States and others have begun moving ahead aggressively since 1999 to address HIV/AIDS in Africa. Paradoxically, this shift ushers in both significant opportunities and stark hazards.

Most positively, HIV/AIDS has risen globally on the foreign policy agenda of major bilateral, multilateral, and corporate actors. Both U.S. leadership and U.S. public opinion are now focused on the need to do more, and better, on an urgent basis. The same can be said for UNAIDS and the World Bank. (In September 2000, the latter announced the new $500 million—now $750 million—Multi-Country HIV/AIDS Program for Africa, intended to expedite funds for prevention, care, and treatment programs, with special emphasis on elementary care capacity in local communities.) Two other organizations, the G-8 and the UN, called attention to the Africa HIV/AIDS pandemic at meetings in 2000. In May 2000, roughly coincident with the president's executive order, five major pharmaceutical manufacturers—GlaxoWellcome, Boehringer-Ingelheim, Bristol-Myers Squibb, Merck, and Hoffman-La Roche—announced that they were prepared to negotiate 70 percent to 90 percent discounts in the price of AIDS drugs sold in Africa. Merck and the Gates Foundation subsequently announced at the July Durban AIDS conference a joint $100 million comprehensive HIV/AIDS intervention partnership with the government of Botswana to strengthen prevention, health care access, patient management, and treatment. This followed the prior announcement in 1999 by Bristol-Myers Squibb of $100 million in assistance to southern African states over a five-year span.

In the spring of 2001, prices for antiretrovirals fell precipitously, essentially to the level of production cost, under the pressure of adverse publicity, generic producers, NGO activists, and the loss by pharmaceutical corporations of their lawsuit against the South African government.

This momentum creates opportunity for leadership. If seized energetically and realistically, the Bush administration can take conscious advantage of a nascent bipartisan consensus in Congress to support expanded engagement against HIV/AIDS in Africa and elsewhere. If focused upon the compelling moral, humanitarian, and transnational security interests at stake, the administration could seek action on a phased plan of steadily increased commitments that has a reasonable chance of achieving modest demonstrable results in the near term while laying the groundwork for the long-term effort that will be needed to reverse this epidemic. The administration could begin to make the case that enhanced mobilization of donor political will and resources could eventually close the gap between current resource levels and projected requirements for prevention and treatment in Africa. Such action would demonstrate what is feasible in the near future for other regions acutely threatened by the pandemic.

Present worldwide spending for both prevention and care in Africa is approximately $1 billion, of which the U.S. contribution is approximately 50 percent. UNAIDS estimates that, at a minimum, the need for elementary prevention, care, and treatment in Africa for HIV/AIDS stands at $3 billion (not allowing for any antiretroviral medications). More detailed calculations by USAID, based on UNAIDS data, estimate that annual aggregate shortfalls could exceed $4 billion. USAID estimates that annual prevention requirements in Africa amount to $1.2 billion to $2 billion to achieve a 25 percent reduction in new infections over the next five years. Annual requirements for elementary care are estimated at $1.8 billion to $2.9 billion: to provide the minimum means to ease the suffering of millions and begin to mitigate social, economic, and political strains, even as the needs of the ill, their families, and orphans steadily mount. These are rough, baseline estimates of what is required to begin to register meaningful concrete impacts. Far higher estimates will be required to begin increasing access to antiretroviral treatments. UN secretary general Annan, in his address to the Abuja summit in late April 2001, estimated annual costs, if antiretrovirals are included, at $7 billion to $10 billion.

Building upward from the current annual $1 billion level is attainable, providing there is an effective multilateral mobilization of resources and a phased approach. That will only happen, however, if there is U.S. leadership, given the global leadership position the United States has already established for itself on HIV/AIDS.

These figures must be seen in the broader context—of the epic human stakes in Africa and the comparative commitments made by the United States and other major donors to support, for instance, the humanitarian intervention in Kosovo (U.S. contributions there now exceed $13 billion). In this light, the down payment required of the international community to create a prevention and care platform in Africa is neither excessive nor impossible.

In its first four months in power, the Bush administration, after a few early stumbles, did begin to take advantage of the rising international momentum on HIV/AIDS and the opportunity to demonstrate continued U.S. leadership. High-level officials acknowledged the transnational security threat posed by HIV/AIDS. The White House appointed Scott Evertz as director of the Office of National AIDS Policy and announced that policy coordination and leadership would be the responsibility of a task force cochaired by Secretary of State Colin Powell and Secretary Health and Human Services Tommy Thompson. The U.S. Trade Representative indicated that the May 2000 executive order on pharmaceuticals would remain U.S. policy. In early May, President Bush committed $200 million as a down payment toward a global trust fund, and shortly thereafter Secretary Powell visited Mali, South Africa, Kenya, and Uganda, at each stop making HIV/AIDS a priority focus.

Certain risks will have to be factored into any future strategy if U.S. policy is to achieve concrete results in coming years. Weak or absent health infrastructure, incomplete data, and proliferating violent crises will block access and divert attention and resources from the HIV/AIDS crisis in many African nations.

AIDS is an inherently volatile, complex human tragedy that increasingly touches African lives at every turn. It focuses public attention upon private behavior, African leadership, state deficiencies, sovereign sensitivities, and stark inequities between north and south. The widely shared sense within Africa that external observers often invoke shame or blame can quickly poison dialogues. A diversity of responses from African leaders should be anticipated, including confrontation borne of frustration.

President Thabo Mbeki's recurrent statements questioning the link between the AIDS disease and HIV, widely criticized at Durban's international AIDS conference in July, spawned an escalating international and domestic controversy. South African statements in mid-October signaled a backing off from these positions. Nonetheless, this conflict raises the issue of whether, in the critical next few years, South Africa and outside players can move beyond antagonism and mistrust to an effective, higher-level collaboration focused on achieving ground-level results—in the continental leader that has the largest number of people in the world living with HIV and AIDS (4.2 million persons), acute racial sensitivities and a complex history surrounding HIV/AIDS, and a sophisticated scientific and medical community. If there is failure on this strategic challenge, the prospects for effective action on HIV/AIDS throughout Africa will be diminished significantly.

As the human and other costs of HIV/AIDS mount, more political confrontations should be anticipated: these will both test international resolve, and equally important, reveal what level of commitment individual African leaders are prepared to make to combat HIV/AIDS, as their part of a partnership with international donors.

U.S. leaders can reasonably anticipate that African leaders will repeatedly turn conversations to the question of how far the outside world is prepared to go to cover the gap between Africa and the West (a similar line of questioning will emanate from Asia, the Caribbean and Latin America, and other acutely affected areas outside Africa). Will the West invest in health infrastructure, provide substantial debt relief, and promote affordable access to antiretroviral medications, palliative care, and the means to combat opportunistic infections? The argument that the West is adept at spelling out what is required but grossly deficient in delivering essential resources in a timely, meaningful, or sufficiently generous fashion will undoubtedly arise. All of these issues figured prominently at the special Organization of African Unity (OAU) Summit on HIV/AIDS that Nigerian president Obasanjo hosted in April 2001. All of them require persuasive answers.

Up until now, few African leaders have been prepared to attack HIV/AIDS as a strategic national threat. The disease remains a highly sensitive subject in many cultures, emerges slowly, and, in early phases, often affects marginalized segments of the populations that have little power. At the September 1999 UN-sponsored AIDS conference in Lusaka, not a single head of state, including Zambian president Chiluba, appeared. With luck, Nigerian president Obasanjo, former South African president Mandela, and others may soon begin to surmount this roadblock.

The pace at which expanding resources are introduced will have to take careful account of the weak administrative capacity of governments and nongovernmental organizations (NGOs). Donors will also have to be careful not to spread the scope of action too thinly, losing sight of core priorities such as reducing behavior that contracts and spreads HIV. Similarly, if antiretroviral medications are introduced too quickly—without adequate attention to training and infrastructure—that could generate new drug-resistant strains of HIV that would threaten a new epidemic and existing HIV/AIDS programs not just in Africa but Europe, North America, and elsewhere.

On access to pharmaceuticals, mistrust and uncertainty between the major corporations and African governments continue to bedevil efforts to implement corporate commitments to provide discount pricing and project-based assistance. Similarly, many African countries oppose the $1 billion facility on offer from the Ex-Im Bank, arguing that it will result in higher external debt levels.

The precipitous fall in pharmaceutical prices in spring 2001, along with the anticipated drop in the cost of palliative medications, not only changed the basic landscape with respect to cost, international momentum to provide treatment, and the attention paid to pharmaceuticals versus prevention and urgent care priorities. It also carried into a new phase the international debate over what balance to strike between the protection of property rights and ensuring affordable access to critical pharmaceuticals and other medical technologies. Pharmaceutical corporations continue to argue that measures such as parallel importing and compulsory licensing will undermine patents, reduce profits, and reduce incentives to invest in future research and development of new drugs. Activists, within the U.S. government and without, continue to press for public subsidization of research, deep price reductions ("tiered" pricing for health emergencies), and selective local manufacturing. One important risk is that pharmaceutical corporations may conclude that there is little profit in Africa and in development of future HIV/AIDS medications and disengage from Africa and other areas acutely affected by HIV/AIDS. Another risk is that discussion of the way forward could become entangled in the ongoing U.S. domestic debate over affordable prescription drugs for seniors and others. It will be critical in the next few years to ensure that, in Congress and the media, the debate over domestic and international medical costs not become framed as a budgetary tradeoff—between effective action against HIV/AIDS in Africa and elsewhere outside the United States and the interests of ill or vulnerable populations in the United States.

In the midst of these uncertainties, the Bush administration, Congress, and other donors will puzzle over various questions—how much assistance makes best sense, for what specific purposes, through what mix of bilateral and multilateral channels, and on what schedule? Pressures will build in Congress and elsewhere to demonstrate results and leverage contributions from other donors, most of whom have contributed only modest amounts. As the pandemic takes root more visibly in Asia and areas of the former Soviet Union, attention could be pulled away from Africa, especially if, in the next few years, there is not convincing proof that an enlarged external investment can bear significant results.

In sum, the next several years offer a window of opportunity for building broad support around a robust engagement on HIV/AIDS in Africa. With care, the Bush administration can capitalize on the present international momentum to do more, urgently, to provide the support necessary for HIV prevention and care.

RECOMMENDATIONS

To effectively combat HIV/AIDS in Africa, the new administration is best advised to concentrate its attention on several priority areas.

■ *Clarify policy goals, specify concrete outcomes, and strengthen the organizational capacity to lead.* Coherent, high-level, unified leadership within the U.S. government on the international aspects of the HIV/AIDS epidemic has been lacking even as the United States routinely asks affected countries to ensure such leadership is in place as a first step to address the epidemic.

Often, it has not been clear how policy is to be coordinated. National policy on international AIDS has often not been clearly spelled out—either for internal or external purposes—and insufficient work has been done to mobilize and coordinate with other donors. Embassies and USAID missions are not routinely staffed to monitor and advance a global U.S. HIV/AIDS policy. High-level Washington travelers to Africa do not carry a consistent policy message on HIV/AIDS. In future years, a coherent and effective U.S. approach will require high-level attention from departments and agencies that are just now becoming active programmatically on HIV/AIDS.

The new administration will be far better equipped to lead if it coherently and forcefully establishes early on—for an internal interagency community as well as a U.S. and international audience—its top priority policy goals for HIV/AIDS for the coming years. That would entail devising a multiyear strategic approach that clarifies how HIV/AIDS policy fits within overall U.S. foreign policy goals, ties its aims to feasible concrete results and adequate resources over the long term, and carefully defines reasonable standards of success or failure.

Especially important will be clarifying the scope of the administration's commitment to build health infrastructure and enhancing access to drugs for palliative care and treatment of opportunistic diseases as well as to antiviral drugs against HIV. The administration will also need to define the assistance needed from other donors as well as other U.S. departments and agencies, including the Departments of Defense, Commerce, Labor, the intelligence community, and the U.S. Trade Representative's Office. It will be important to address, as a matter of U.S. foreign policy, the continued stigma attached to HIV/AIDS, the human rights risks that people living with AIDS confront, and the need for proactive international measures to strengthen protection. So long as people living with AIDS remain threatened, many will go underground, only worsening the public health challenge of reaching this population in a timely and effective way.

Recent progress has surmounted organizational weaknesses in Washington, including the decision by the Clinton administration in September 2000 to designate the director of the White House AIDS Office as President Clinton's special envoy on global HIV/ AIDS, and the subsequent decision by the Bush administration to appoint Scott Evertz as director of the Office on National AIDS Policy and to establish a task force on HIV/AIDS cochaired by Secretaries Powell and Thompson. However, much additional work remains to ensure effective leadership and coordination. Interagency lines of authority still need to be clarified, just as emergent key staffing requirements need to be filled—in technical program implementation, managing the interagency process and relations with Capitol Hill, and international negotiations. Early in its tenure, the Bush administration should systematically weigh its options, decide upon a course of action, and move quickly to implement it.

■ *Match resources to goals, for a long-term plan.* The Clinton administration and Congress jointly agreed in 2000 to substantially increase resources; additional corporate and foundation resources are coming; and the Bush administration has moved to increase FY2001 levels ($464.5 million) by 10 percent in FY2002 and committed an additional $200 million to a global trust fund. A yawning gap still exists, however, between official rhetorical aims and the resources now at hand, even as new resources continue to be allocated on an emergency, ad hoc basis.

The Bush administration compact—with Congress, other major powers, and international organizations—will be essential to bring resources quickly into alignment with the projected estimated requirement to advance scientific research, prevention, care and treatment, and vaccine development. As noted earlier, no less than an additional $3 billion a year—and more realistically more than $4 billion—is required in Africa to bring down infection rates and provide basic treatment, care, and support for orphans. That figure could double if antiretrovirals are factored in. In the immediate term, a reasonable U.S. contribution would be at least $1.5 billion a year, phased in over the first two years of the Bush administration. That would more than double current U.S. commitments.

If the U.S. government is to leverage cooperation from Africa, donor nations (Japan, Australia, and Europe), and multilateral partners, it has little choice but to mobilize substantial new U.S. foreign assistance reliably over an extended period. That will require careful balancing: to ensure that rising U.S. commitments truly leverage others and will not in fact create disincentives for others doing more. This objective would best be achieved through a phased course of action, pressed aggressively early in the new administration. Only after the United States has moved beyond ad hoc adjustments to strategic planning of resource commitments will uncertainty about the sustainability of U.S. efforts and potential resource trade-offs with other vital foreign policy purposes decline.

■ *Launch sustained high-level initiatives that advance collaborative partnerships.* Early and regular high-level administration travel to Africa, with an HIV/AIDS focus, will be essential. The new administration will need an aggressive plan to leverage other bilateral donor commitment levels comparable to U.S. commitments. To restructure the global public health architecture, U.S. diplomacy and resources will be needed to strengthen UNAIDS in Geneva, utilizing that mechanism to erect new cross-continental partnerships with activist African leaders, international organizations, G-8 partners, and non-African countries facing rising AIDS challenges. A key element will be anticipating and responding effectively to denial, obstruction, and backlash. U.S. policy should anticipate, and respond constructively to, rising assertions in Africa of sovereign autonomy and control over programs, resources, and knowledge. Early in the new administration, special attention should be paid to ensuring that the international dialogue with South Africa enhances cooperation and minimizes confrontation.

- *Accelerate and expand essential activities that work.* The Durban international AIDS conference confirmed that there is considerable knowledge, embodied within the emerging international consensus, of what essential activities now need to be brought to scale (e.g., testing and counseling facilities, mother-to-child transmission programs, public awareness campaigns, treatment of sexually transmitted diseases, expanded access to cost-effective drugs for palliative care, and the treatment of related or opportunistic diseases). The challenge now is to mobilize resources, identify reliable governmental and nongovernmental partners, and maintain focus over the long term on the core interventions that change risky behavior and reduce HIV transmissions, mitigate suffering, and strengthen national capacities.

  Part of this will also involve giving priority to public-private pilot programs—incorporating governments, NGOs, and pharmaceutical corporations and other private industry—to improve access to a range of medications as well as training and other infrastructural requirements. More retrospective analysis of behavioral interventions is also needed to ascertain which programs have the greatest impact and are the most cost effective, particularly in changing behavior within high-risk populations that contract and spread HIV. Long-term efforts should also include programs to advance and disseminate scientific knowledge and build the capacity of African scientists and laboratories to conduct research on HIV infections, HIV vaccines, prevention and care strategies, and the interconnection between HIV, other infectious diseases, and poverty. The United States should continue to press for prevention and treatment strategies that are both scientifically validated and culturally appropriate.

- *Strengthen U.S. understanding of the interrelationship between AIDS, development, and security.* New applied analyses should be undertaken in several priority areas: which economic sectors in Africa will be most heavily affected by AIDS; how international investment patterns and interregional trade will be altered; what changes are foreseen in household incomes and consumption patterns; and which areas and populations nutritional status will deteriorate most sharply. In each of these, new bilateral and multilateral programs will likely be required.

The approaches taken by the Department of Defense and intelligence agencies to internal, regional, and transnational security threats will require updating. New models will be needed to address weak and failing states that come under grave new strains from AIDS and lack effective infrastructure to deliver health care or guarantee elementary security. More, not less, state failure and violent insecurity is projected, which will translate into new forms of transnational security threats. How these threats unfold, how precisely AIDS fuels them, and how they can best be mitigated within and outside Africa is at present only poorly understood.

■ *Refine international trade rules on key drugs.* In developing vaccines and better, cheaper antiretrovirals, microbicides, and other medical technologies, the U.S. private sector has a dominant global position, and these are the areas where continued U.S. official leadership can pay off.

The new administration should continue refining national policy—in concert with the G-7, WTO, World Health Organization, and UNAIDS—regarding pharmaceuticals and medical technology, especially on tiered pricing, parallel importing, compulsory licensing, and subsidization of research. Tough controversies will persist over balancing competing imperatives: how to protect international property rights and ensure adequate future investment in research and development versus ensuring affordable access to emerging humanitarian emergencies. The United States, through the NIH, FDA, and other agencies, has significant sway over biomedical research and the development and licensing of treatments: this gives the Bush administration special opportunities—and responsibilities—to lead in seeking pragmatic and workable solutions for future international trade rules on pharmaceuticals.

CONCLUSION

HIV/AIDS is a complex human tragedy that is devastating Africa and expanding infectious disease threats globally. However, there is hope that a concerted international effort can bring down new infection rates and expand access to care and treatment. To achieve success will require the essential element of U.S. leadership—to take full advantage of bipartisan congressional interest and converging international opinion on the urgency to act and to press a long-term strategic approach.

CHAPTER THREE

U.S. DIPLOMATIC STRATEGIES
TO RESOLVE CONFLICTS IN AFRICA
Terrence P. Lyons

IN THE 1990S, AFRICA'S MULTIPLE AND EXPANDING CONFLICTS proved highly resistant to diplomatic resolution, gravely strained Washington's capacities, and reversed hard-won developmental gains and democratic reforms. Crises in Africa threaten U.S. interests: they generate vast humanitarian suffering and human rights abuses, including genocide, and invite terrorism, endemic disease, drug trafficking, and environmental degradation. Ignoring these conflicts will create tensions with important allies, disrupt U.S. relations with the United Nations, and provide openings for rivals like Libya and China. U.S. bilateral influence in Africa has waned in the post–Cold War era—despite unprecedented high-level attention from the Clinton administration—and Africa's urgent crises threaten to keep top-level U.S. officials from attending adequately to conflict prevention and peacebuilding.

Faced with these daunting challenges, the Bush administration should take several steps to ensure a coherent, feasible diplomatic strategy. Effective diplomacy requires systematically rebuilding U.S. diplomatic capacities in Washington and in key embassies. It requires articulating explicitly to Congress, the media, and interest groups U.S. interests in curbing conflict in Africa. It requires selectivity and toughness: specifying priorities and defining objectives, benchmarks, and robust incentives and disincentives the United States is prepared to deploy, including support to peacekeeping operations. It requires focused leadership in those cases where U.S. leadership can have a decisive and positive impact—in this study's opinion, in Eritrea-Ethiopia, Sierra Leone, and Zimbabwe. It requires active, vigilant, but discreet engagement in the regionalized war in the Democratic Republic of Congo (DRC) and in Sudan's civil war, where U.S. policymakers must seek, in cooperation with allies and multilateral organizations, new ways to engage and put effective pressure on the parties to these conflicts to bring an end to war, and create some credible basis for a sustained and just peace. In other conflicts and crises-in-the-making, it will require engaging broadly and ensuring diplomatic readiness. Overall, effectiveness will require mobilizing new international coalitions through sharply heightened senior-level engagement with European and African allies. As a rule, policymakers should avoid raising expectations with grandiose rhetoric and focus instead on pragmatic actions to promote peace. A realistic, selective approach has a reasonable chance, by the end of 2004, to contribute to the successful resolution of two to three crises and help arrest or contain other threatening situations.

In Eritrea-Ethiopia, the signing of a peace agreement in December 2001, encouraged by critical high-level U.S. engagement and support for UN peacekeeping, represents a major breakthrough and should receive priority attention to finalize implementation and support the longer-term peacebuilding process. Zimbabwe will demand priority attention and support for Africa-led preventive diplomacy, if a worsening crisis, which could destabilize South Africa and other parts of southern Africa, is to be forestalled. In Sierra Leone, Great Britain has taken on a critical leadership role in promoting a fragile peace process and deserves significant support from the next administration, bolstered by continuing support to UN peacekeeping and regional involvement.

In Sudan and the Democratic Republic of Congo, new dynamics are emerging since the Bush administration took office, and there are opportunities in Sudan where more intensive, high-level engagement by the United States can have a positive impact. By mid-2001 the Bush administration had laid down the broad outlines of a policy to promote a negotiated, just peace in Sudan, but doubts remained as to whether this approach could attract sustained support from Congress and interest groups, particularly hard-line elements that strongly preferred a policy of containing and pressuring Khartoum while committing lethal and nonlethal support to the southern opposition.

In other chronic crisis areas, such as Burundi, Angola, and Somalia, where peace processes are flagging or moribund, continuous diplomatic engagement is warranted but at a lower profile and on a more realistic basis. What is required is adequate readiness and quick response when opportunities to promote peace appear, or alternately, when these crises veer toward interethnic violence with massive human rights abuses that could reach genocidal proportions.

THE NATURE OF THE CHALLENGE

In 2000, the United States was engaged to a greater or lesser degree in efforts to manage or resolve a broad range of African conflicts.

In Sierra Leone, the United States played an important role in pressing the Sierra Leonean government to accept the Lomé peace agreement. Following a return to war by the insurgent Revolutionary United Front (RUF) and Foday Sankoh, Great Britain took a lead role and sent troops to bolster the forces defending Freetown. Washington supported this initiative, accepted an expanded UN peacekeeping operation, and offered military training to Nigeria and other West African forces to improve the capacity of regional troops to enforce the peace. U.S. envoy Jesse Jackson traveled to West Africa a number of times to push for peace, Under Secretary Thomas Pickering traveled to Liberia to pressure Charles Taylor to break his links to the insurgents, the effort to support Nigeria's involvement in peace enforcement was a major topic during President Clinton's trip to Abuja in August 2000, and Sierra Leone remained high on the United Nations agenda.

More recently, the United States and the United Kingdom successfully led a UN motion to impose a diamond and arms embargo on Liberia, intended to cut off the RUF's lifeline, and there is evidence that these sanctions (along with the presence of UK troops) are paying off with the rebel disarmament process continuing apace as of

June 2001. Continuing U.S. engagement, including support for efforts under way at the UN to establish an independent Special Court in Sierra Leone, is critical to the peace process, to British and Nigerian policymakers, and to the future of UN peacekeeping.

The devastating war between Ethiopia and Eritrea finally ended in a fragile peace agreement in December 2000. U.S. special envoy Anthony Lake played an instrumental role in mediating with Organization of African Unity (OAU) representative and Algerian president Abdelaziz Bouteflika to move both sides to accept the Algiers accord, an important example of successful cooperation to manage a peace process. The United Nations, with U.S. support, deployed a peacekeeping mission that is essential to the Algiers accord. The accord is an important opportunity to build peace, but success is not guaranteed, particularly given an uncertain political situation in Addis Ababa and deep divisions within Eritrea and within Ethiopia's ruling party over the accord. Implementation and rebuilding peaceful relations between the two states will require deft diplomacy, U.S. leadership, and resources in the course of the Bush administration.

One of the most complex ongoing conflicts is in the Democratic Republic of Congo, where a devastating, multisided civil war is complicated further by the intervention of Zimbabwe, Angola, Namibia, Rwanda, and Uganda. The DRC has seen some of the continent's worst violence and threatens to be a source of protracted instability and a platform for conflict between and within neighboring states. The United States provided diplomatic support to the Lusaka peace process, applied pressures on late DRC leader Laurent Kabila to accept Botswana's former president Ketumile Masire as a mediator, and supported a phased UN peacekeeping operation. Ambassador Richard Holbrooke traveled to the region in 1999 and 2000 and placed significant focus on the crisis during his tenure as president of the UN Security Council. The United States also helped engage Uganda and Rwanda in talks that led to their withdrawal from the area around Kisangani. In early 2001, Laurent Kabila's death set off a new but still uncertain political dynamic that has led internal and regional actors to reassess their positions, thereby creating the potential for a new push for peace. The central issue is whether the Lusaka accord remains a viable framework and whether other alternative subagreements within Congo and among the regional armed interveners are urgently needed. The scale and potentially destabilizing consequences of this nearly continent-wide war makes it critical for the Bush administration to find a way to press more effectively for peace and to stand ready with significant resources if a peace process gains traction.

The protracted and tragic conflict in Sudan has created one of the largest and most difficult humanitarian crises in the world. The Clinton administration adopted a posture that identified Sudan as a "rogue state" and supported Ethiopia, Eritrea, and Uganda as "frontline states" to contain Sudan. Human rights issues, notably slavery and religious persecution, became highly salient to a variety of U.S. advocacy groups, making Sudanese policy closely scrutinized in Washington. In 1999, the United States appointed a special envoy, Harry Johnston, and worked with its European allies (most notably Norway and Italy) to support a peace process under the auspices of the Intergovernmental Authority on Development (IGAD). The IGAD process has shown only meager results since adopting an important Declaration of Principles in 1993, and it has become clear that a new, extraregional process will be necessary. Political changes in Khartoum and within the opposition National Democratic Alliance raise the prospect of a new political dynamic with the potential for either escalation or de-escalation.

A vocal and diverse coalition of domestic U.S. constituencies on Sudan has pushed the Bush administration early on to come up with a strategy on Sudan. Secretary Powell visited Nairobi and Kampala in May 2001 and announced that the U.S. would provide $60 million in humanitarian assistance to persons in need in both the north and south, that a special envoy would soon be announced to contribute to an international effort to reach a negotiated, just settlement to Sudan's war, and that the United States would pursue an even-handed approach to bring pressures and inducements to bear upon both Khartoum and southern opposition.

In Burundi, the United States supported the Arusha peace process, initiated by former Tanzanian president Julius Nyerere and continued by former South African president Nelson Mandela. Special Envoy Howard Wolpe engaged in a large number of meetings and discussions with regional leaders, representatives of concerned governments and institutions in Europe, and a wide range of groups in Washington. President Clinton flew to Arusha to attend a signing ceremony in 2000, but although a limited agreement was signed, a number of actors—most crucially the principal armed groups—remain outside of the peace process.

Other serious ongoing conflicts include Angola and Somalia. In these two cases, after earlier periods of intense but ultimately frustrating and unsuccessful engagement in peace processes, Washington stepped down its involvement. In Angola, following the collapse of the Lusaka peace agreement, the impetus shifted to military efforts by the regime in Luanda to defeat UNITA in the field and by the international community to isolate and apply sanctions against UNITA. Angola remains a significant source of oil imports to the United States, and several U.S. companies have significant investments there. If the conflict were to end, massive tasks of peacebuilding and reconstruction will remain for a country torn apart by decades of brutal internecine warfare. In Somalia, after the withdrawal of UN forces and a period of mixed violence and localized order, a peace conference sponsored by Djibouti took place in 2000. Washington monitored events, but policy analysts concluded that high-level U.S. support was not justified, partly because they viewed the process with skepticism and partly because they believed such support would complicate the initiative. If peace in either of these cases develops momentum, the Bush administration must be prepared to support implementation and long-term peacebuilding and reconstruction.

Three important states are at risk of precipitous decline into violent conflict and deserve concerted effort by Washington to prevent escalation.

Zimbabwe in particular poses significant risk owing to its rising internal tensions, its role in the DRC conflict, and its importance to South Africa and the region. In 2000, the situation in Zimbabwe deteriorated sharply, with the launch of government-backed invasions of white-owned commercial farms in March and widespread violence in the lead-up to the June parliamentary elections. The United States registered deep concern over the erosion of the rule of law, suspended support to the government's Land Reform and Redistribution Program, and appealed to other donors and Southern Africa Development Community (SADC) member states to assist in ending illegal occupations and violence. But these actions were hardly bold, and the United States has missed several key opportunities to influence change in Zimbabwe, particularly in pushing for a withdrawal of Zimbabwean troops from Congo. Compared with the European Union (EU), which was unstintingly frank in its criticisms of the election process, the United States maintained a relatively low-profile, listless approach in dealing with Zimbabwe.

Secretary of State Powell's stinging rebuke of President Mugabe, delivered on May 25 in Johannesburg, marked a radical shift in the U.S. approach. In forging a comprehensive strategy of conflict prevention, the Bush administration should continue to give Zimbabwe priority attention.

The December 1999 coup in Côte d'Ivoire, in which General Robert Guei overthrew the regime of Henri Konan Bedie, marked the onset of a period of instability, violence, and economic uncertainty that, if unchecked, will have serious economic, political, and demographic implications for Cote d'Ivoire's neighboring states. Many Ivoirians question the legitimacy of President Laurent Gbagbo, and his victory rapidly disintegrated into political and ethnic fighting between his supporters and those of rival opposition leader Alassane Ouattara. In this case, the United States has limited leverage and should instead seek to engage early on and at high levels with French policymakers, who hold greater political and economic sway. Further, the United States should commend efforts of regional organizations, like the OAU's "Committee of 10," which confronted General Guei in the preelection period. The United States should build on and encourage similar undertakings.

Kenya will present the Bush administration with serious policy challenges in the long run-up to the 2002 elections. Slow, steady decline is expected to continue, and possibly accelerate, as elections draw nearer and economic pain intensifies. A complicating factor is that President Daniel arap Moi is precluded by Kenya's constitution from seeking a third elected term. Corruption is intrinsic to Moi's clientelist regime, and curbing corruption will be a formidable task that will require fundamental political change. The Clinton administration's official policy of promoting democratization and economic reform was basically sound, but implemented inconsistently and viewed, among Kenyan opposition groups, as confusing and irresolute.

Finally, there is a further category of states where the potential for violent conflict requires intensive engagement to consolidate peace. The most important state in this category is Nigeria (discussed elsewhere in this study), where the success or failure of the democratization process will be critical to the prospects for peace and stability in West Africa. The threat of renewed war in Liberia and instability and violence in Guinea could seriously undermine the peace process in Sierra Leone, and the risk of regionalized war is growing. Continuing conflicts in parts of Uganda and Senegal could escalate. The process of consolidating peace in Mozambique continues to require attention. The list is long, and each case has its own risks and complicated dynamics. These "watch list" cases require diplomatic engagement to prevent conflict and have the potential to escalate, arguing for high-level diplomatic attention from Washington.

CLINTON'S ENGAGEMENT WITH AFRICA

The Clinton administration paid unprecedented attention to conflict resolution in Africa. President Clinton himself traveled twice to Africa. He made an important speech on the Rwandan genocide during his first trip and, on his second trip, consulted with Nigerian officials on Sierra Leone and threw his office and personal prestige behind Nelson Mandela's efforts to reach an enduring settlement in Burundi. Under Secretary of State Thomas Pickering, U.S. ambassador to the United Nations Richard Holbrooke, former NSC adviser Anthony Lake, and Assistant Secretary Susan Rice each became deeply engaged in the quest to reverse Africa's proliferating crises. Multiple special envoys were appointed for Africa.

Paradoxically, in this period of high-level attention, U.S. working-level capacities declined and U.S. bilateral influence waned. Early in the Clinton administration, the Department of State's Africa Bureau lost a deputy assistant secretary of state position and 60 officer positions. Increasingly in the 1990s, the Africa Bureau and embassies in Africa could not fill important lower and mid-career positions; typically more than 25 positions have been vacant. A large number of mid- and senior-level officers migrated out of the Africa Bureau. Large stretches of the continent—particularly areas suffering acute conflict—are no longer regularly covered by on-site diplomatic personnel. These include Sudan, eastern Congo (where an enormous humanitarian crisis rages largely unseen), northern Nigeria, Angola (outside of Luanda), and Somalia. The closure of more than a dozen USAID missions in Africa and comparable cutbacks in intelligence resources further undermined U.S. capacities to manage conflicts. Today, U.S. embassies in Abuja, Harare, and Abidjan, to name but the most conspicuous, operate at substandard strength. The United States has had no functioning embassy in Khartoum since early 1996.

Clinton foreign policy relied heavily upon special envoys, in part to compensate for worsening shortfalls in senior personnel available to manage crises. In the Great Lakes and Liberia, envoys proved valuable in coordinating actions with neighboring states, Europe, the United Nations, and diverse interest groups in Washington. Envoys also effectively supported UN peacemaking in Angola and provided crucial mediation in the Eritrea-Ethiopia border war. However, envoys also carried costs and risks: at times they eclipsed the authority of ambassadors and Washington-based officers; had weak, overly narrow mandates; were perceived as empty, symbolic gestures; received inadequate backup from Washington; and were inadequately integrated into the upper reaches of decisionmaking.

The Clinton administration also identified a number of African heads of state as the "new leaders" and accorded them special status: Meles Zenawi, Isaias Afewerki, Yoweri Museveni, and Paul Kagame. At important points during the Eritrea-Ethiopia border war and the Congo crisis, close identification with these leaders conflated their interests with U.S. interests and compromised Washington's standing in Africa. At the same time, hardened hostility toward others (e.g., the late Congolese president Laurent Kabila and the National Islamic Front government in Khartoum) limited contacts, access, and tactical maneuverability.

Taking sides in conflict is not inherently inadvisable. The question is how deftly and effectively these alliances are leveraged to advance U.S. interests, and how well the United States defends itself against manipulation that runs counter to U.S. interests. In retrospect, U.S. identification with "new leaders" brought few benefits and many disadvantages. A hard-line, condemnatory approach to Khartoum, combined with a high rhetorical alignment with the southern opposition, yielded no apparent gains in ending Sudan's 18-year war and achieving a credible peace settlement. It remains to be seen whether these inherited, strained partnerships can be put to better use by the Bush administration.

In this same period, the Clinton administration supported several Africa-led peace initiatives: the ECOMOG-managed Abuja process in Liberia and Lomé negotiations for Sierra Leone, the Nyerere- and later Mandela-led Arusha process for Burundi, the IGAD initiative for Sudan, and the Africa-led Lusaka process for Congo. Up to now, these "African solutions for African problems" have been weak, highly flawed, and prone to breakdown. None has generated a durable, coherent accord. For each, the challenge now is to define how to move forward, preserving gains achieved in prior negotiations while avoiding stasis.

The Clinton administration's collaboration with European allies on Africa was a decidedly uneven effort. Relations and coordination with Great Britain were critical to policy toward Liberia and Sierra Leone, particularly in 2000, and Special Envoy Howard Wolpe consulted regularly with his counterparts from the European Community and Great Britain on the Great Lakes crises. But in other areas, coordination lagged. The United States and its allies failed to develop common policies toward the crisis in Central Africa and allowed the "troika" (the United States, Russia, and Portugal) to languish with regard to Angola. Washington and Europe never agreed on the most effective policy toward the conflict in Sudan, and rivalry between Paris and Washington complicated international policy toward Rwanda and Burundi.

BUILDING AN EFFECTIVE DIPLOMATIC STRATEGY

The Bush administration will face chronic and emergent crises that are resistant to diplomatic interventions and that threaten recurrent massive human rights abuses. Africa's crisis agenda grew to immense proportions during the Clinton years: state collapse in Somalia and Sierra Leone; genocide in Rwanda; endemic interethnic violence in Burundi; a failed peace process in Angola; complex peace implementation tasks in Mozambique, South Africa, and Liberia; regionalized wars in the Democratic Republic of Congo and Sudan; the Ethiopia-Eritrea border war; smaller but complex crises in the Central African Republic, Chad, Guinea, Guinea-Bissau, Lesotho, and Senegal. Democratic transitions in South Africa and Nigeria, two key regional powers, have been fragile, and three important regional states— Kenya, Côte d'Ivoire, and Zimbabwe—now teeter on the brink of potentially dangerous collapse.

Choosing one or two crises to engage intensively at a high level does not mean that the United States should entirely ignore other African crises. This strategy is extremely hazardous. First, as Rwanda and Sierra Leone have demonstrated, the United States will pay a significant price in its ability to assert global leadership if a conflict that has been neglected explodes. An administration that ignores the threat of genocide and other forms of mass violence against civilians imperils its position in the world. Second, the Bush administration will inherit a legacy of U.S. involvement in many of these conflicts that will be difficult to ignore and commitments that cannot be withdrawn without damaging relations with key allies and institutions. The future of UN peacekeeping will be shaped in large measure by the outcome of complex peacekeeping and peace enforcement operations already launched with Washington's support in Sierra Leone, Ethiopia and Eritrea, and the Democratic Republic of Congo. Disengagement is not an option for a global power with global interests.

FOCUSED LEADERSHIP

In some cases, the United States can and should accept a leadership role and pursue it with vigor and determination. Sierra Leone, Ethiopia-Eritrea, and conflict prevention in Zimbabwe deserve special attention and should be priorities for resources. In each case, the stakes are high, U.S. credibility is on the line, and diplomatic progress is both possible and essential to forestall costly regression to violence.

The scale and brutality of the conflict in Sierra Leone places it in the forefront of global humanitarian and human rights agendas. The UN (with active British leadership) now struggles to implement the largest peacekeeping operation worldwide, at the same time that the United States has committed to a multiyear "train and equip" program for Nigerian and other West African battalions. The UN peacekeeping operation has been in crisis and Washington should work to provide the resources and incentives to encourage troop-contributing states. The United States has endorsed a war crimes tribunal and imposed limited sanctions against Liberia for its role in contributing to the conflict. Increased efforts to control the diamonds-for-guns networks are necessary, and UN efforts in Angola demonstrate the potential for such initiatives in West Africa. A renewed political negotiation, though highly problematic, will be essential to guarantee progress in Sierra Leone and avoid a slide back into violence, war crimes, increasingly regionalized war, and international recriminations.

The Ethiopia-Eritrea border war had enormous human costs and significantly damaged stability in the Horn of Africa. The accord that was signed in Algiers demonstrates the value of sustained high-level U.S. engagement, tied to reliable senior Algerian partners, the OAU, and the UN, and backed by a package of credible incentives and tough disincentives, including support for a UN peacekeeping operation. Intense follow-on diplomacy is now required to bring to closure several key outstanding issues and begin the longer-term process of building sustainable peace in the region. Washington should capitalize on its considerable investment in the peace process and play a leadership role in supporting peace implementation. In addition to

UN peacekeeping, supported financially and with a handful of symbolic U.S. military observers, the United States should support demobilization, regional arms control, and projects to reinvigorate economic activity and other regional linkages.

Zimbabwe's worsening crisis threatens the stability of South Africa and the broader southern Africa community. A nascent international coalition is forming—out of the ad hoc efforts of South African president Thabo Mbeki, Nigerian president Olusegun Obasanjo, and UN secretary general Kofi Annan—that holds promise but has yet to reverse Zimbabwe's slide toward economic collapse, internal violence, and regional instability. Given the stakes, the Bush administration should work assiduously to focus a coalition around a feasible agenda that will have constructive, meaningful effects on Harare and the opposition.

BROAD, VIGILANT ENGAGEMENT

Although diplomatic engagement is necessary across a broad range of crises, no single country, even a great power, can or should take a leadership role in every case. In some cases a given peace process has bogged down and displays little potential to succeed. The IGAD peace process in Sudan and the Lusaka process in the Democratic Republic of Congo have struggled to develop momentum in the face of deeply rooted conflicts where mediators lack sufficient leverage over key parties to the conflict. Some of Africa's conflicts may not be ripe for resolution, and careful analysis and diplomatic engagement are required to determine if additional opportunities can be developed and seized. Washington should keep its distance from moribund processes or cases where it lacks leverage while remaining vigilant for openings to encourage a more effective process.

In Sudan, it is time to devise a framework to supersede the IGAD process, retaining the important Declaration of Principles agreed upon in 1993. Similarly in the Democratic Republic of Congo, the policy of pressing parties to the conflict to accept the Lusaka process is unlikely to yield sustained, satisfactory results, and a more realistic, pragmatic framework will need to be established to complement

Lusaka. In some of these cases other states or organizations will be better positioned to play a leadership role, and the United States should encourage and reward them for doing so. But the Bush administration should refrain from using regional peace initiatives as an opportunity to strike a pose and make public pronouncements supporting a process that has little prospect of success. Instead, Washington should adopt a posture that is lower in profile but diplomatically vigilant and seeking to develop more credible opportunities.

A diplomacy of broad engagement to promote conflict resolution entails a watchful vigilance that seeks to explore and expand opportunities for more assertive action. In cases where the conflict is not yet ripe for resolution, U.S. diplomats should actively seek leverage over the parties and develop incentives and sanctions to encourage peace. Regular discussions with a full range of actors in the region as well as with allies in Europe and international organizations are important to build a sense of common purpose and to construct an effective, multilateral approach. Advance planning and identification of resources will position the United States and its allies and partners to move quickly and decisively when openings arise.

In a number of cases, conflicts in Africa have become regionalized, as neighbors intervene to pursue their own agendas. This is particularly the situation in central Africa, where interlinked conflicts cut a swath across Angola, Congo-Brazzaville, DRC, Rwanda, Burundi, Uganda, and Sudan, but is increasingly becoming the case in West Africa, where instability and violence in Sierra Leone, Liberia, Guinea, and Côte d'Ivoire feed off each other. In such regionalized conflicts, diplomats and special envoys should seek to encourage neighbors to disengage, respect borders, and work to establish peaceful relations. Engaged diplomacy should also look to the broader structures of arms flows and the trade in diamonds and other resources that provide the wherewithal for parties to the conflict to continue engaging in violence.

The conflict in the Democratic Republic of Congo is a case where full-blown U.S. leadership is at present unlikely to yield tangible results, but where vigilant and robust engagement is absolutely essential. The scale of the conflict, the ongoing massive human rights abuses, the potential for genocide, and the threat to expand and further destabilize the region compel an active U.S. diplomatic engagement to develop a more effective peace process. The African-led and U.S.-supported Lusaka peace process has thus far achieved very little, because the main parties have not been seriously committed to implementation, and distrust and lack of capacity have disabled the regional security architecture of the Joint Military Commission. Since the death of President Laurent Kabila and the accession to power of his son, Joseph, some positive movement by the DRC government and the intervening forces has occurred.

But implementation of the Lusaka agreement and the launch of the Inter-Congolese Dialogue will remain fraught with uncertainty. The Lusaka Ceasefire Agreement points to the need for both a regional security arrangement and a process for internal Congolese conflict resolution and may serve as a reference document for a broader peace process. The conflict resolution agenda in Congo should shift to underscore diplomatic rather than peacekeeping issues and should emphasize the regional and political economy dimensions of the conflict. Key decisions relating to Congo are likely to be made in Rwanda, Zimbabwe, and Angola, and the United States should actively seek to create incentives and sanctions to encourage Congo's neighbors to support peace. Leaders in neighboring states should be told that their commitment to an effective peace process will be scrutinized when decisions are made regarding aid, debt relief, and trade agreements. The conflict has spawned serious and widespread human rights abuses and violations of international humanitarian law. To achieve lasting peace and security, the administration must work in collaboration with the international community to make accountability a fundamental component of U.S. policy. The United States also should aggressively seek to create an international regime to manage the diamond and gun flows that feed the conflict, building on the important work done under UN auspices with regard to Angola and Sierra Leone. This will require deft diplomacy to gain the cooperation of other international powers, most notably Russia and China.

In Sudan, the Clinton administration's high-profile strategy did little to advance the cause of a negotiated peace, and in this instance, as in DRC, a lower-profile approach as part of broader multilateral collaboration offers a better chance of progress. The administration stressed the aim of containing and isolating Khartoum through routine condemnation, high-level official travel to opposition groups in southern Sudan, and bilateral and multilateral sanctions. A secondary goal was to end the war through support of peace talks held by an ineffectual, fragmented regional body. Ultimately, the administration's high rhetoric and its efforts to isolate Khartoum did little to weaken the Sudanese government, strengthen the opposition, or promote a process of genuine peace negotiations. Instead, as European states and Sudan's neighbors steadily normalized relations with Khartoum, the United States found itself in conspicuous self-isolation, with few achievements to show for its efforts.

In Sudan, U.S. policy should focus explicitly on the single overriding objective of ending the war, a goal that offers the best means to see positive change in areas where U.S. interests are at stake—putting an end to mass human suffering, pervasive human rights abuse, economic decay, and the export of terrorism. A multilateral approach that involves key European and regional states will be most effective in pushing the parties to the conflict to the negotiating table. The United States will clearly be essential to the establishment of a new international nucleus dedicated to ending the war, but need not in this case chair the coalition or be always on the front line of the effort. The United States should instead position itself to provide active support to collaborative leadership by other extraregional states—for example, Norway and Britain.

The United States will face international and domestic pressures to undertake a leadership role in one or another of these crises. Important regional states will push for U.S. leadership, such as South Africa in Congo and Burundi and Egypt in Sudan. Important constituencies within the United States will advocate action. The horror of genocide in Rwanda will keep human rights concerns high in the Great Lakes, as will the massive human rights abuses in Sudan, Angola, and Sierra Leone. Indeed U.S. diplomats should remain actively engaged with these conflicts and seek to develop opportunities and expand openings for viable peace processes. But in the face of moribund peace processes, other areas deserve higher priority to ensure that limited resources can be concentrated where they can best make a difference. Rather than spreading resources thinly and ineffectively, the Bush administration should concentrate its efforts in a few cases and engage them intensively.

CRISIS PREVENTION

The scale and complexity of managing large-scale crises should not divert attention and needed resources from the equally complex and potentially more rewarding challenges of crisis prevention. Special attention must be given to those states where large-scale conflict has not yet broken out, but where precipitous decline into violence is imminent. Zimbabwe, Côte d'Ivoire, and Kenya represent states that deserve particularly close monitoring and policies to encourage conflict prevention. In all three cases, relatively small amounts of timely, strategically deployed resources could prevent a damaging conflict from escalating into a major crisis.

In these cases, the United States must engage key partners aggressively in a multilateral approach. In Côte d'Ivoire, it must particularly attempt to put aside tensions and mutual recriminations with the French and seek to consult and coordinate policy with top-level French policymakers. In Zimbabwe, Washington should work closely with African leaders and organizations to put effective pressures on the government to reassess its dangerous policies of fomenting violence for political purposes. The United States should also work to bolster efforts by African states and organizations—ECOWAS, SADC, and the OAU—to exert influence on intractable leaders.

Finally, the administration should seek to broaden and deepen bilateral engagement to support democratization, civil society, and rule of law. Such support should emphasize institutionalization and capacity building and seek to encompass a broader range of civil society groups, both rural and urban. The administration should make a concerted effort to mobilize and leverage U.S. domestic groups like the Corporate Council on Africa, the American Bar Association, the National Democratic Institute, the International Republican Institute, and the International Foundation on Election Systems. The United States should continue its support for democratic elections, maintain long-term engagement in the electoral process, work to strengthen legislative and judicial bodies, and engage key actors at the regional and local levels to support democratization. The U.S. Agency for International Development could play a key role—perhaps through the Office of Transition Initiatives—to help quell potential violence and work toward national reconciliation and resolution of ethnic and religious divisions.

WHAT WILL THIS STRATEGY REQUIRE?

The Bush administration must, as a first priority, increase the human resources available for diplomacy toward Africa. The complexity of tasks relating to Africa justifies the return of the deputy assistant secretary position and other foreign and civil service officer slots lost earlier in the 1990s. Special envoys serve as important tools in specific cases but need administrative support and should not be regarded as a substitute for increased human resources within the Africa Bureau and embassies in Africa. Additional resources and incentives are needed to encourage foreign service officers (particularly mid-level officers) to bid on jobs in Africa. The closing of USAID missions in many African countries and the lack of sufficient intelligence resources to monitor developments have made it extremely difficult to mount an effective strategy to respond to, much less anticipate and prevent, conflicts. The lack of on-site personnel is particularly damaging in Africa because the continent lacks the media coverage, Internet connectivity, and regular flow of scholars and business people that supplement official reports in other regions of the world. More strategic engagement with expertise and organizations outside of government can provide broader and different perspectives, improve analysis, and increase the capacity of U.S. diplomacy.

With declining U.S. bilateral leverage in Africa and a growing realization that the United States cannot and should not play a leadership role in every African conflict, the Bush administration should make the most of its alliances with key European and African states. U.S. policy on conflict resolution in Africa needs to be made a regular, sustained part of broader policy agendas in transatlantic relations, relations with key African allies, and policy toward international organizations. International legal frameworks to combat transnational crime and limit the flow of guns and resources that support conflicts make close multilateral collaboration even more essential. European states and institutions often have resources and flexibility in certain areas that the United States lacks. What is needed is systematic, institutionalized engagement with U.S. allies in Europe and with the European Union. Such consultations and coordination are necessary before crises emerge to ensure a common understanding of issues and interests at stake. A bilateral meeting with Paris is a particular priority, but more important than any single meeting is the establishment of a regular series of high-level consultations. A number of U.S. embassies in Europe have designated "Africa watchers" to maintain contacts, facilitate policy coordination, and report on African issues. These positions should be replicated in U.S. embassies in Europe and elsewhere. Greater attention should be paid to the African policies of China, Libya, Malaysia, Brazil, and other states whose role on the continent has increased as Western powers have reduced their involvement.

When the United States does decide to take on a leadership role in ending African conflicts, it must have the ability to apply credible pressures on actors who hinder peace and to offer adequate incentives to encourage peace. The international community recently has recognized the links between resources and conflict and has taken preliminary steps to try to limit the guns-for-diamonds networks that feed conflicts in Angola. The work by the Fowler Commission to mobilize international pressure on actors who assisted UNITA despite UN sanctions demonstrates the potential for more consistent pressure to isolate parties that contribute to conflict. Such efforts should be supported and expanded to Congo and West Africa. Additional efforts are needed to increase pressures on leaders such as Charles Taylor in Liberia to end their support for combatants who refuse to accept negotiated agreements or to pressure the Bashir government in Khartoum to end the war in southern Sudan. Further efforts to limit the availability of small arms to conflict zones, reduce the use of landmines that kill civilians and obstruct postconflict rehabilitation, and to promote justice in cases of war crimes and other massive human rights abuses will provide additional levers to encourage parties to accept peace.

The Bush administration should develop a pool of resources that can be used to move parties toward peace in Africa. Current levels of expenditure are clearly insufficient and dramatically restrict the ability of U.S. diplomats to play a meaningful role commensurate with the challenges. In addition to increasing the overall level of resources, the administration must not allow these expenditures to become overly encumbered in other, broader agendas, thereby diminishing their effectiveness for promoting peace. The Bush administration should continue to follow the Clinton administration's lead in recognizing that one component of meaningful aid to promote peace is serious, professional engagement with African militaries through mechanisms such as the African Crisis Response Initiative and the African Center for Strategic Studies. Mechanisms for quick dispersal of assistance, such as those in USAID's Office of Transitional Initiatives, should be expanded in order to seize opportunities to encourage conflict resolution. Serious and creative initiatives to limit the flow of guns and resources that support conflicts should be emphasized.

CONCLUSIONS

The Bush administration faces a daunting set of challenges relating to war and violence in Africa. Many ongoing peace efforts will need high-level attention quickly. The United States should engage broadly in diplomatic efforts to encourage peace processes in Africa. To pursue an effective diplomatic policy requires investment in human resources within the Africa Bureau and embassies and a greater coordination with allies. Beyond broad diplomatic engagement, the Bush administration should selectively take a leadership role in several conflicts where opportunities exist and the stakes are high. As argued above, implementation of the Ethiopia-Eritrea peace accord, support for a peace process in Sierra Leone, and proactive leadership to head off potential crises in Zimbabwe deserve priority consideration. The crisis in Central Africa needs creative engagement to encourage conditions for a viable peace process. Effective engagement in these cases will require resources to develop additional leverage over parties to the conflict in the form of targeted incentives and credible sanctions.

The Bush administration should place priority on the following:

- *Rebuild capacities and create readiness.* The U.S. capacity to engage broadly and routinely in conflicted areas—its readiness to respond to diplomatic openings and threats of violence—rests on U.S. embassies and on the State Department's Africa Bureau staff in Washington. The secretary of state should announce early that an urgent departmental priority is to revitalize diplomatic capacities in Washington and key embassies in Africa. Special incentives, exemptions, and other exceptional personnel measures should be formulated. A fourth deputy assistant secretary position should be restored. Special envoys, used selectively, should be guaranteed adequate administrative backup, clear and authoritative mandates, and high-level access in Washington. Such enhanced capacity will improve Washington's ability to monitor peace processes vigilantly and to act decisively when opportunities arise to advance peacemaking.

- *Set priorities.* Intensive high-level engagement, backed with adequate resources, should be focused on Sierra Leone, Zimbabwe, and advancement of the Eritrea-Ethiopia Algiers accord, where U.S. stakes are considerable, where a credible or promising negotiating context exists, and where the costs of breakdown would be high. For each, a robust interagency strategy should clarify goals, benchmarks, incentives, and disincentives. Policymakers should avoid spreading meager resources too thinly and should concentrate their efforts in a set of priorities where U.S. leadership can make a difference. For Washington to play an effective role in these priority areas, additional and more flexible resources—carrots and sticks—to increase leverage over the parties to the conflict are necessary. In Sudan, the administration should pursue a multilateral, concerted effort to end the war. In Congo, the administration should explore the use of region-wide sanctions or embargoes to curb the flows of arms and diamonds that fuel the war and should work toward establishing a dialogue among the major parties to the war—Angola, Zimbabwe, Rwanda, Uganda, and DRC—that will lead to a new, sustainable regional security compact.

■ *Win higher congressional investment in peacemaking.* High-level, continuous dialogue with Congress will be essential to guarantee political support for the administration's conflict resolution policies, expand flexible, quickly disbursed peace-support funds, enlarge transitional programs, contribute to UN peacekeeping forces, and offer bilateral support to African peacekeeping forces. Congressional support will also be important in devising punitive measures applied against spoilers.

■ *Mobilize new international coalitions: leverage existing African partnerships, strengthen collaboration with South Africa and Nigeria, and revitalize transatlantic alliances.* The Bush administration should structure its dialogue with African leaders around concrete goals and expectations related to priority conflicts (e.g., ending the Eritrea-Ethiopia border war, reducing instability and violence in the Congo, and promoting peace in Sudan and Somalia). Early on, and at a high level, it should open a dialogue with South Africa, Nigeria, and major European powers on how to create new, dynamic international coalitions that can bring concerted incentives and disincentives to bear on parties to priority crises. Washington should institutionalize diplomacy relating to conflict resolution in Africa within its relationships with multilateral and international organizations.

CHAPTER FOUR

U.S. INVESTMENT IN SECURITY OPERATIONS IN AFRICA
Jendayi E. Frazer and Jeffrey I. Herbst

WITH THE NOTABLE EXCEPTION of the Ethiopia-Eritrea border war, the United States has failed to exercise leverage effectively to end Africa's wars. Yet because virtually every U.S. interest on the continent is affected by conflict, the U.S. response to Africa's wars will profoundly affect the entirety of U.S. policy toward Africa. Africa is home to a disproportionate number of the world's conflicts, public order is breaking down in many countries, and the popular conception that Africa is plagued by conflict is increasingly correct. The Bush administration will face ongoing conflicts in West Africa, the Horn, and genocide-prone Central Africa, as well as the prospect of significant unrest in Côte d'Ivoire, Kenya, and Zimbabwe. Inevitably, investment in security operations looms large in U.S. foreign policy debates on Africa.

It is clearly in the national interests of the United States to address African security problems in a coherent manner rather than resorting to ad hoc arrangements once fighting has begun. The United States spends considerable resources each year responding to the human costs of war, including refugees and famine, and conflict is antithetical to virtually every U.S. policy goal. War in Africa undermines U.S. interests in economic development, democracy and human rights, the provision of education and basic health care services, and stemming the HIV/AIDS pandemic. None of these issues can be adequately addressed where basic public order is not assured. And when conflicts in individual African countries leave tens or hundreds of thousands dead and wounded, destroy states, and destabilize entire regions, Africans, Americans, and the world at large will inevitably ask what the lone remaining superpower is doing about a particular war. Moreover, terrorists, like Usama bin Laden, and international criminal networks take advantage of Africa's conflict-ridden areas to base their operatives and threaten U.S. global interests. Finally, the necessity of a clear U.S. policy toward Africa's wars is especially urgent given the continued weakness of the United Nations and the limitations of Africa's regional organizations in responding to conflict.

Investment in peace operations should not become a substitute for policy or diplomacy. The new administration should put together comprehensive policies that treat security as a worthwhile deliverable in the context of enhancing overall state capacity, including support for the rule of law and civil society. Meaningful and consistent consultation with Congress and the American public will be essential in building support for an overarching, coordinated military and non-military engagement plan. Realistically, regional initiatives cannot soon replace international peacekeeping efforts. Peace operations will only improve if the United States takes the lead in mobilizing transatlantic allies, as well as willing and capable African states, to move beyond crisis response to prevention and peace enforcement. However, European allies and African lead states will only heed U.S. calls for involvement if it is clear that the United States is prepared to match its rhetoric with high-level political engagement and significant material commitments.

Two peace operations require sustained attention and will be critical test cases in determining the future of UN and regional peacekeeping operations in Africa. The problematic, contentious operation now under way in Sierra Leone will require substantial U.S. support. The recent U.S. initiative to train and equip up to seven West African battalions (including five Nigerian battalions) for peacekeeping in Sierra Leone has met with resistance by Nigerians, who criticize the program's conditionalities, elementary curriculum, and resource levels. The Bush administration, which has signaled that it is willing to carry the program forward, should take steps early on to bolster this program and devise a support framework that is mutually acceptable to both Americans and Nigerians. The Ethiopian-Eritrean peace settlement is another case in which the United States has made a considerable diplomatic investment and should do its utmost to ensure that the UN peace operation, which is integral to the peace accord, is implemented expeditiously. Although the United States does not lead in this situation, it should put full diplomatic support behind the United Nations and European lead states and fulfill its commitment to providing technical and logistical support.

A third UN operation, in support of the Lusaka peace agreement for the Democratic Republic of the Congo, began to move forward in its deployment in early 2001, following the death of Laurent Kabila. This effort was significantly aided by Secretary Powell and other senior officials in the Bush administration through encouragement of the Congo's internal dialogue and pressures upon intervening states, most notably Rwanda and Uganda, to begin withdrawal of their forces from Congo. This operation will merit continued high-level diplomatic support.

A LOOK BACK: THE CLINTON ADMINISTRATION'S POLICIES AND PROGRAMS

The Clinton administration's rhetoric toward Africa, especially during the second term, stressed the significant U.S. commitment to the continent. Yet, U.S. policy was noticeably reactive and, in spite of promises of high-level engagement, did not appear to be framed within a broader strategy or vision for Africa. For almost all of the first Clinton administration, Somalia dominated official thinking, to the point that the United States violated its own international legal obligations by not intervening to combat the genocide in Rwanda that began in April 1994. Responding to the coup in Burundi in mid-1996 and fearing another genocide like Rwanda's, but still unwilling to place U.S. forces in Africa, the administration publicly considered the creation of an African Crisis Response Force (ACRF), a proposal that called for creating a rapid response African capability for continental peace and humanitarian operations. The ACRF concept was soon abandoned, however, for lack of congressional support or consensus within the administration for what appeared as a standing army under U.S. leadership. Potential European and African allies were also opposed because they had not been consulted in advance of the U.S. announcement of the proposed force.

With the second Clinton administration, a more nuanced strategy had evolved. The ACRF was renamed the African Crisis Response Initiative (ACRI) and limited to providing training and nonlethal equipment to several African countries. ACRI was then further limited by Congress to providing traditional peacekeeping ("chapter six") training only, rather than the more robust peace enforcement ("chapter seven") training that was obviously needed for most African conflicts. Moreover, it was underfunded at $20 million for the first year. It also was not possible for ACRI to benefit several of Africa's most capable armies. Washington ruled out Kenya, Angola, and Nigeria (up until the advent of the Obasanjo government) out of concern for political and human rights and eventually ruled out Ethiopia, Uganda, and Rwanda because of interstate wars. Inversely, South Africa ruled out cooperation with Washington owing to a perceived lack of prior consultation by Washington and unresolved questions about how the force would actually operate and under whose authority and control. As a result, smaller, less capable forces (e.g., Ghana, Malawi, Senegal, and Benin) were the recipients of ACRI assistance. After spending close to $100 million on ACRI, it is unclear what the United States has to show for its efforts.

The Clinton administration also continued modest forms of traditional U.S. bilateral military outreach, including $8.5 million per year for International Military Education Training (IMET) for African troops, one or two annual West African Training Cruise (WATC) ship visits, and fewer than 20 Joint Combined Exercise Training (JCET) events each year for all of sub-Saharan Africa. For several years, the administration provided ad hoc assistance to support Nigerian peacekeepers that totaled $110 million—mainly for a U.S. security company's logistical contract to airlift West African peacekeepers to areas of operation. Finally, the African Center for Strategic Studies (ACSS)—conducting a series of civil-military seminars for senior African military leaders—was established in 1999 and funded at $40 million for five years.

The United States also contributed to UN peacekeeping operations in Somalia, Rwanda, Angola, and Mozambique. It shouldered about 30 percent of the international community's total cost of more than $5 million. Results, except for the Mozambique operation, were ambiguous and largely disappointing. Since 1999, new UN peacekeeping operations in Sierra Leone, Democratic Republic of the Congo (DRC), and Ethiopia-Eritrea have placed an additional burden on the limited global Contributions in Peacekeeping Account (CIPA).

Even this activism by the second Clinton administration was no match for the rhetoric of senior officials and was clearly inadequate in light of the wars that broke out in the 1990s—notably, in Angola, Liberia, Sierra Leone, and Ethiopia-Eritrea, and the constellation of conflicts in the Great Lakes. As a result, a significant aspect of U.S. policy toward African conflicts was multilateral diplomacy that urged both European and African countries to do more—more than the United States was willing to do—and particularly encouraged African regional groupings like ECOMOG to commit troops to peacekeeping efforts. Despite an increase in resources for ECOMOG, ACRI, and bilateral support to approximately $800 million, there was little noticeable change in any of Africa's wars. The Bush administration must assess whether efforts to shape the African strategic environment through ACRI, ACSS, IMET, WATC, and JCET are misguided, inadequately resourced, or simply need more time to bear fruit.

A LOOK FORWARD: AFRICA'S HOT SPOTS

The Africa that the Bush administration confronts remains riddled with wars. Each of the wars is prompted by unique local circumstances, but many have spilled across regional borders, creating "conflict systems" (notably in West Africa, the Horn, and Central Africa) that defy purely domestic solutions. The Bush administration will face several conflicts that will call for immediate attention, but are fraught with risks—both for the United States and for Africa.

Sierra Leone

Decisively ending the brutal civil war between the democratically elected government in Sierra Leone and the Revolutionary United Front will demand significant U.S. leadership. The decision to send several hundred U.S. soldiers to Nigeria to train up to five West African battalions, at a cost of $90 million in fiscal years 2000 and 2001, for deployment in Sierra Leone associates the United States more publicly and directly with an African war than at any point since Somalia. It represents an important evolution in U.S. foreign policy at the end of the Clinton administration, providing more robust training and direct engagement with Nigeria, whose military is one of Africa's most capable. Yet the resources furnished thus far, although significant, are less than what is required for Nigeria to become a reliable and competent leader in West African peace operations. The United States must confront the possibility that training and the modest amount of equipment provided to the West African forces does not result in a decisive turn in the Sierra Leone war. Calls for a more robust engagement may follow, especially as demands increase for the senior leadership of the RUF to face an international tribunal. It is uncertain what form such engagement should take.

At the same time, fighting the RUF may mean killing a large number of child soldiers, which will highlight the moral ambiguities of any involvement in Sierra Leone. Also, troops trained by the United States could possibly be involved in significant human rights abuses in Sierra Leone and might, given the large Nigerian contingent, conceivably intervene in politics in their home country. Under such circumstances, current congressional support would almost certainly evaporate, absent a clear articulation of U.S. interests and a well-reasoned appeal for public support. In particular, a consistent and coherent message of why it matters to train and equip African forces is critical.

Democratic Republic of the Congo

The Bush administration faces demands to enhance funding and support for the UN peacekeeping mission to DRC. The Congo conflict has mutated into a series of conflicts involving the government in Kinshasa, armies of at least five other countries, and several proxy groups operating in loose federation with one or more of the national armies. Peace negotiations have been uneven, and only in early 2001, following the death of Laurent Kabila, did Congo's internal dialogue and the withdrawal of foreign forces inch forward, along with the deployment of almost 1,000 UN peacekeepers by mid-2001. It remains uncertain whether the signatories of the Lusaka agreements are genuinely committed to full implementation of the accord. The possibility that conflict may ignite on a number of fronts cannot be ignored. An international force to promote peace in DRC can have enormous benefits if successful but will face continued hazards. The modest UN operation will encounter many more armed groups and individuals than in Sierra Leone, with as much or more incentive to fight, in a territory some 20 times as large, with few roads. Should the conflict intensify, the sheer number of troops required—at least 50,000 to be effective—likely rules out fielding an international force. Even so, the Bush administration will face sustained international and domestic pressure to exercise leadership in the Great Lakes, where the potential for mass violence and genocide is high and where economic opportunities and strategic priorities in the mineral-rich Congo loom large.

Ethiopia-Eritrea

As a result of the Clinton administration's prominent role in the Ethiopia-Eritrea ceasefire negotiations, the United States will probably be asked to maintain a flow of logistical equipment and technical assistance to enhance the UN peacekeeping force in the Horn. The two-year Ethiopian-Eritrean war that ended in December 2000 resulted in tens of thousands of dead (perhaps 70,000 on the Ethiopian side alone) and set back development for both countries. At one level, fielding such an interpositional peacekeeping force as the one there is relatively easy because the United Nations has considerable experience with this kind of "chapter six" intervention. Yet, genuine peace between Ethiopia and Eritrea—which requires rebuilding mutual trust and confidence—will remain elusive for a generation. Both countries' armies are disciplined and answer to their civilian leaders, but, regardless of the intentions of the governments, if fighting were to resume, the consequences could be disastrous not only for Ethiopians and Eritreans, but also for UN peacekeepers.

The three conflicts above are especially important because they will inevitably flavor the Bush administration's posture toward conflict in Africa, much as Somalia determined the Clinton administration's Africa policy for the following seven years. An administration that responds on an ad hoc basis will resort to half-hearted measures designed to counter the "CNN factor," a reactive posture that will court disaster. On the other hand, even a modest peacekeeping success would provide ammunition for domestic constituencies that favor a more prominent U.S. role in African conflict resolution. Correspondingly, outright failure could guarantee that the United States will not invest in peace operations for another four years. Thus, the new administration does not have the luxury of a learning curve.

Other Conflict Areas

Another set of wars will inevitably demand U.S. attention early in the new administration's tenure—that is, the brutal and seemingly endless conflicts in Angola, Burundi, Somalia, and Sudan. Some or all of these may, at one time or another, lurch toward some kind of resolution, possibly requiring outside peacekeepers. At that point, they will become high on the U.S. agenda, as demands for U.S. support—in dollars and soldiers—become significant.

Finally, a number of African countries not currently at war could spiral toward civil conflict during the next four years. The most likely and significant are Côte d'Ivoire, Kenya, and Zimbabwe, all once prosperous countries, driven to the brink of collapse by incompetent and venal leaders. Conflict prevention efforts that include facilitating negotiations, offering incentives, and threatening sanctions will be the key to immediate U.S. diplomacy in those countries, but the need to respond to large-scale violence cannot be ruled out over the long term. Any number of other African countries, including, but not limited to, Cameroon, Chad, Congo-Brazzaville, Ethiopia, Guinea, Guinea-Bissau, Lesotho, Liberia, and, most important, Nigeria, are plagued with political instability that may erupt into conflict in the next four years. The Bush administration will have at its disposal only limited intelligence assets in Africa, which will undermine U.S. ability to forecast future trends and discern the internal dynamics of conflicts in Africa's fluid strategic environment. The low priority given to official collection and analysis of African issues has made the U.S. government reliant on other governments, private business, academics, and especially NGOs and journalists for good information.

Although it is hard to predict exactly where hot wars will break out next in Africa, it is almost certain that they will. The security situation on the continent as a whole has changed dramatically since 1993 when the Clinton administration took office. Interstate wars have emerged, and African governments are increasingly willing to undertake direct military intervention into neighboring territory, rather than rely on proxy rebels. All of the "internal" wars in Africa have a regional component, as neighbors feel compelled to intervene to help one of the protagonists or because the flow of guns, drugs, and refugees from war-torn countries threaten to overwhelm fragile neighboring states. Thus, the demand for investment in security operations will outstrip what even an extremely activist U.S. administration will likely be able to supply. A realistic assessment of available resources is needed, given that previous and current resource levels are grossly inadequate for the situations found on the ground. Moreover, a triage strategy may be called for if the total demand for African security operations continues to exceed what all prospective donors (including other governments' bilateral security programs and UN-funded programs) are willing or able to supply.

THE DOMESTIC LANDSCAPE

The domestic landscape will also be difficult for the Bush administration. Attitudes toward intervention in Africa reflect the great tension that has riven U.S. foreign policy for two centuries. On the one hand, there is an instinctive desire and long tradition on the part of the American people and many different constituencies in Washington to alleviate extreme suffering. At the same time, there is a profound and well-founded skepticism that outsiders, especially Americans, can make things better during most civil wars and a suspicion that the United States often makes things worse. This division was arguably intensified by the Clinton administration's strong rhetorical commitment to ending conflicts and its simultaneous reluctance to put any Americans in harm's way. There is a profound skepticism within Congress and the U.S. military itself about how involved the United States should become in security operations in Africa. Finally, ongoing domestic debates about race will inevitably raise the question of a double standard as U.S. forces are deployed when European lives are at stake but stand by when massive killing and genocide occur in Africa.

The American public's desire to help in times of emergency is sufficiently strong and the forces irreversibly opposed to intervention sufficiently inchoate that the next administration will not find pleas to Congress to fund investment in security operations dead on arrival. However, it must be absolutely clear that any case that commits U.S. dollars and U.S. troops (even in a supporting role) to an African conflict will have to be fully supported and pressed by the highest-ranking officials in the administration. An assistant secretary of state for African Affairs—no matter how knowledgeable and competent—will not be able to make the case to Congress alone. Camouflaging interventions by pretending that they are cheap and that U.S. soldiers will not be involved will be met with great skepticism. Keeping investments in security operations low profile may get one or two through the U.S. political system, but when things go wrong (as they almost inevitably do), the failure to prepare fully may cause support for all future operations to evaporate. The administration must be prepared to make a compact with Congress: it will only propose interventions in Africa with the utmost seriousness, and Congress, for its part, must be prepared to review these operations with equal gravity.

The Bush administration must communicate the hard facts of African peace operations to the American public; unfortunately such operations are seldom easy or clear-cut. One of the great lessons of Somalia is that there can be no such thing as a "surgical" humanitarian strike. Exit options are rarely quick or easy. Even if peace emerges in a particular country, it may be years before ex-soldiers find work, guns are returned, and politics are normalized. And until these things happen, a return to violence is always a possibility. Exit options are seldom clear in most conflicts—a fact not lost on Congress and a key barrier to U.S. intervention. Indeed, announced exit plans can serve as a roadmap for the fighters who live in the country to wait out the peacekeepers and resume battle. Thus, most interveners who have any positive effect on a country tend to stay far longer than they originally anticipated. It is of course possible for external interveners to conduct an operation limited in scope and in time, but only if they are prepared to leave the country in question responsible for rebuilding the political and economic institutions—and risk more violence and humanitarian problems.

As a result, clarity of vision, competence, and long-term commitment are critical to peace operations in Africa. Unfortunately, operations tend to be planned poorly, staffed in an ad hoc manner, lacking in a clear roadmap for action, and rife with conflicting motives among the various armies that make up a given peacekeeping force. The administration will need to convince the American people that strong U.S. leadership is necessary for African peace operations to go even moderately well, but that U.S. involvement is no guarantee of success. Because interventions are long, difficult, and costly processes, they should not be undertaken lightly; prior to a decision to support, there must be hard-headed analysis of the problem and proposed solution, with a reasonable assurance of adequate international political will and material resources for the duration. And there must be a reasonably clear plan leading to an end-state including the gradual, coordinated replacement of military assets with civilians.

A NEW APPROACH TO SECURITY OPERATIONS IN AFRICA

The Bush administration will not have the luxury of time to become familiar with the lay of the land in Africa before being faced with a crisis. It will need to shorten dramatically the learning curve for effective action to reverse the growing skepticism of both Americans and Africans toward U.S. willingness to be part of the solution to at least some wars in Africa. Strategic foreign policy planning early on will help prevent U.S. policy and programs from languishing for an extended period to the detriment of U.S. interests in Africa.

The rhetoric during the Clinton administration tended to suggest active involvement in all of Africa's conflicts. However, rhetoric and good wishes are never enough in any war. Only a change in the situation on the ground, propelled by the introduction of money and peacekeepers, will make peace at least possible, although not necessarily likely, in many African conflicts. Thus, for internal political reasons as well as exigencies in the field, the Bush administration should significantly ratchet back its rhetorical commitment to be constructively involved in every African conflict. The administration must make clear that it is willing and able to be guided to choose its spots by strategic U.S. interests—for example, to protect resident U.S. citizens and U.S. facilities and maintain access to secure lanes of communication (sea, air, and land) and to oil and other strategic resources. And, once it has chosen to intervene—with money, trainers, or troops—the administration must be adamant that it will be cognizant of the risks, resolved in its efforts at the highest levels to explain its position to Congress and the public in order to win their support, and resolute in carrying out its policies. A simple test (in the most extreme case of deploying troops) will be whether the new administration so justifies a program that the death of one or more U.S. soldiers does not automatically derail the intervention. Congress and the public must be sufficiently convinced of an intervention's worth and importance so that even the spilling of American blood can be understood within a greater humanitarian and strategic context.

When the administration determines that U.S. national interests are at stake in a particular conflict, it should be prepared to deploy adequate resources to get the job done. Although Africa is a relatively insignificant theater of operations, the United States can still bring significant resources to bear there. U.S. contributions to African security operations sometimes amount to only tens of millions of dollars, sometimes less—only a fraction of what the United States will often spend on humanitarian relief in countries shattered by war. At the same time, the United States has significant military assets—including airlift capability, logisticians, reconnaissance, and communications—that could be deployed, given domestic consensus, resolve, and budgetary resources, without quite bringing U.S. troops into combat.

The Bush administration needs a clear vision of why the United States is involved in Africa and needs to devote far more attention to promoting coordinated actions among the different agencies, departments, and commands so that this vision can be realized. A U.S. administration with resolve should be able to eliminate many of these bureaucratic and political obstacles and enable the United States to deploy the few resources it will dedicate to Africa in the most effective manner possible. The administration should, for instance, consider options (as part of broader force reorganization planning) to achieve greater operational coherence and meaningful engagement than currently achieved with Africa divided among four combatant commands. This may entail having a designated commander-in-chief for Africa under a geographic command, similar to Korea under the U.S. Pacific Command. The administration should review all U.S. and other foreign security programs, coordinate them so they reinforce one another, and determine if they are adequate. If they are not, the administration should determine how to improve outcomes or cut losses and disengage. Critical to this process will be upgrading all current U.S. intelligence collection postures and requiring agencies to develop the capacity to provide policymakers with the information necessary to make coherent policy decisions. If new resources are not available for African collection and analysis, the administration should require the agencies to systematically obtain information on Africa from companies, research institutions, media, NGOs, universities, and other friendly governments.

It should be realized that clear U.S. leadership in at least some African conflicts is necessary but that leadership must be exercised in coordination with U.S. allies and capable African lead countries. Part of "choosing the spots" should clearly mean that the United States will sometimes have to play a leadership role in African conflicts. The pattern of Sierra Leone, where the United States and United Kingdom worked closely together, should become more of a precedent for all

African wars—although it may be unrealistic to expect other European countries not as closely aligned with the United States to play the cooperative role that the UK did in Sierra Leone. Picking the conflicts where the United States will take the lead will be a delicate question that will depend on resources, circumstances on the ground, the U.S. domestic scene, and consultation with close allies and African regional leaders. The administration should invest time and resources in building partnerships with key transatlantic allies with a view toward strengthening U.S. leverage and sharing the burden of peacekeeping in Africa, where cooperation with other countries is critical for any chance of success. Also critical will be partnerships with key African anchor states that have the ability to lead a coalition of willing states in peacekeeping and peace-enforcement operations.

Moreover, the onset of a crisis is far too late a time for the administration to determine where U.S. interests in the country at hand warrant U.S. leadership or intervention, and too late a time to begin a dialogue with Congress about intervention. Rather, early on in the administration's tenure, congressional representatives from both parties should be briefed repeatedly on the new administration's policies and strategies. Congress will continue to demand that it be consulted on each individual conflict. However, preparatory work with critical congressional leaders will make it apparent that the administration has a coherent policy and is not just striking out in an ad hoc manner. The administration should invest time and resources in building coalitions with key congressional members, committees, and caucuses to build support for UN and regional peace operations as an alternative to placing U.S. forces on African soil.

A significant aspect of U.S. policy must be to develop a long-term and sustainable capacity for Africans and the UN to be able to intervene. Because the United States cannot be involved in all conflicts—and must explicitly say so—it is critical that regional and UN peacekeeping efforts be strengthened. The most important examples of these are in West Africa but it is also possible that the Southern African Development Community will follow through on its commitment to develop its own capacity. Although regional peacekeeping efforts are essential, it is important to recognize that they are not without significant problems. For example, in many instances, African peacekeepers may have an approach to the laws of war that is different from that of the U.S. military. African intervention—as demonstrated by Nigeria's history in Sierra Leone—will be just as political as Western intervention, especially when there is no clear legal authority or decisionmaking framework within the subregional organizations to guide or constrain the behavior of lead states involved in the operation. Indeed, as neighbors, African interveners may have far more immediate interests in the destination country than the United States or the United Kingdom. For this reason, committed regional forces are more likely to stay the course when their troops come under fire and are killed. But the potential for conflicting interests or agendas argues against placing the burden on Africans; a more prudent approach would be to field a coalition force comprising both non-African and African states.

Reliance on regional capacity for peace operations over the short term is not viable, since only ECOMOG (which depends almost entirely on Nigeria) has shown multilateral effectiveness in, or stomach for, regional operations. Although Africans have widely declared their intention to build subregional capacity, it does not yet exist in Central Africa, and East Africa has only nascent capability in the new East Africa Community. The Inter-governmental Authority on Development, with members from the Horn and East and Central Africa, has no collective organizational military capability (although Ethiopia and Eritrea have clearly, if destructively, demonstrated their capacity to project force in the region). Even in West and Southern Africa, regional leadership is not guaranteed as both Nigeria and South Africa have pressing domestic problems.

Thus, building sustainable African peace capacity will require long-term strategic planning and investment. The administration should forge a compact with Congress and the Department of Defense to provide select African lead states with the combat training and equipment required to generate the types of units needed for peace enforcement situations. It should work to build competent national armies with the command and control capacity necessary to conduct successful peace operations and should structure lethal training programs to ensure ongoing human rights monitoring and efforts to protect civilian populations. The administration will need to address explicitly and publicly the trade-offs associated with the creeping practice under the Clinton administration to use private security companies to provide training and logistical support to African forces. The controversial practice is considered by some as providing a cheap, short-term force multiplier for African peacekeeping efforts and by others as encouraging mercenary activities without long-term benefit for building sustainable African peacekeeping capability. The potential cost-saving benefits of using private security companies must be balanced against the multiple government-engagement benefits of official U.S. military personnel directly training and advising African armed forces.

The Bush administration will also have to recognize that the United Nations—for all its problems—is currently the main game in town. For the UN to have any hope of success in these areas requires significant backing from the United States, not only in terms of money but also in political support. As a first step, the United States must reverse the status quo of not paying most of the peacekeeping obligation to the UN and not providing logistics or other assistance except on a cash basis (at three times the commercial rate). Indeed, the United States will undoubtedly have to increase its funding toward UN peacekeeping efforts in Africa if those multinational ventures are to be successful. African peacekeeping operations and underequipped peacekeeping contingents are much less capable than they used to be when the United States paid its bills and provided material support (even if not troops). Moreover, some Africans have not been paid for past peacekeeping operations and are therefore reluctant to participate in new operations, a reluctance that undermines the U.S. strategy to reduce demands on U.S. forces by building UN and regional capacity for peacekeeping.

Through its self-critical reviews of its own actions in Rwanda and Bosnia as well as the 2000 "Brahimi" report on peacekeeping, the United Nations has now provided a comprehensive roadmap for reforming its own peacekeeping operations. It is clearly in U.S. interests to support the reforms suggested. However, rhetorical support for reform will be largely ineffective if the United States does not also materially support the new initiatives. As a first step the United States could sponsor joint exercises with UN contributors, perhaps with specific contributors prior to or just after a deployment, to improve interoperability and work with the UN to improve its peace operation practices, especially enhancing its logistical arrangements, funding options, command-and-control, and headquarters capacity.

CONCLUSIONS

In forging an effective U.S. security policy toward Africa, the new administration should

- *Exercise leadership with allies where immediate progress is possible—and essential.* U.S. leadership in select ongoing operations is imperative, but that leadership must be exercised in coordination with U.S. allies and capable African lead countries. The Ethiopia-Eritrea peace settlement is a clear and immediate case in point. The United States has invested substantial diplomatic resources and energy in the accord and must do its utmost to see that the UN peace operation is carried out successfully. The next administration should put full diplomatic support behind the United Nations and European lead states to provide diplomatic, technical, and logistical support.

- *Pick its spots for future involvement.* In future cases in which the administration decides that U.S. national interests are at stake, the United States should deploy resources up to the limit of its capacity. Today's investment of approximately $130 million in the "150" International Affairs Account for African military and security programs—terrorism, crime, drugs, peacekeeping, conflict resolution, and military education—can only have a modest impact, even in combination with nonmilitary programs. The United States must therefore explicitly attempt to "pick its spots" when it comes to intervention, committing fully to some operations while playing only a supportive role in others. The primary criteria for intervention should be when U.S. interests are at stake and when it appears that the operation will have a reasonable chance of success, especially when it includes the presence of a coalition of African and European partners. The potential for genocide (where the United States has an international legal obligation to intervene), mass violence against civilians, and regional destabilization should figure prominently in calculations of U.S. interests.

- *Reorganize internally existing efforts.* The new administration will need to articulate clearly the reasons for U.S. involvement in Africa and give far more attention to promoting coordinated actions among different agencies, departments, and commands so that this vision can be realized. It should adopt a strategic approach that prioritizes anchor states based on U.S. security interests; consider options to achieve greater operational coherence than is currently achieved with Africa divided among four combatant commands (e.g., designating an African commander-in-chief within a geographic command); review all U.S. foreign security programs and ensure that they are mutually reinforcing; and upgrade current U.S. intelligence collection to provide policymakers with the information necessary to make coherent policy decisions.

- *Provide Congress and the American people with a coherent sense of administration goals and policies in Africa.* The administration should begin early in its tenure to create a congressional consensus and a broad constituency that will work to promote effective engagement in African security operations.

- *Strengthen African and UN capacities.* U.S. policy must develop the long-term and sustainable capacity of Africans and the UN to be able to intervene. The United States cannot be responsible for total external involvement in African security operations and therefore should improve coordination with its European and African allies better to leverage limited resources. In addition, it should enhance the capacity of the UN so that it has a much better chance to bring multilateral peace operations to a successful conclusion. For the first time, it appears that the UN is serious enough about internal reform to justify U.S. activism.

CHAPTER FIVE

CRITICAL U.S. BILATERAL RELATIONS IN AFRICA
NIGERIA AND SOUTH AFRICA
Gwendolyn Mikell and Princeton N. Lyman

As the Bush administration develops its overall Africa policy, strengthening bilateral relations with South Africa and Nigeria should be among its foremost priorities.

First, U.S. effectiveness in Africa demands coherent, reliable, exemplary partners on the continent, and at this time Nigeria and South Africa are the most likely candidates for partnership. Both countries loom large in their regional influence, military capacities, economic sway, and expansive and assertive foreign policy ambitions. Further, both South Africa and Nigeria are important interlocutors in the larger dialogue between the United States and the developing world, whether on debt, control of weapons of mass destruction, trade agreements at the WTO, or drugs. Both these anchor states distinguished themselves in the 1990s through surprising, historic transitions that embraced electoral competition and multiparty governance, respect for human rights, transparency, and reentry into the community of market democracies.

Second, both Nigeria and South Africa, although essential to the future viability of the continent, are nonetheless subject to profound political and economic strains, and hence vulnerable in varying ways to breakdown. U.S. interests lie in mitigating those forces that weaken and put at risk the South African and Nigerian transitions. Both countries have the capacity to lift their entire regions if they succeed and to damage and destabilize them if they do not.

In recent years, South Africa and Nigeria each posed distinct challenges to U.S. policymakers and each elicited distinct policy approaches and outcomes. The Clinton administration was by and large effective with each in seizing opportunities to assist in democratic transitions and in building a solid foundation for future collaboration.

But hard won gains in South Africa and Nigeria are at risk if the United States does not make the necessary investments in coming years, and the Bush administration cannot afford to take current success for granted. Rather it should actively forge stronger collaborative ties and develop innovative new means to consolidate South Africa and Nigeria's complex, unsteady transitions. Achieving workable partnerships on sensitive matters such as crisis management, peacekeeping, economic assistance, and HIV/AIDS will take time; will involve tensions, complex trade-offs, and mutual hesitation; and will not be guaranteed success. Setbacks and frustrations are inevitable. But the reality is that if the United States is to be engaged meaningfully in Africa, it has little choice but to press ahead in testing systematically what is possible in its evolving relations with South Africa and Nigeria.

NIGERIA

Nigeria matters significantly to U.S. national interests. With more than 110 million citizens, it is Africa's largest nation, a regional hegemon essential to security in Sierra Leone, Liberia, and Guinea and to the economies of the surrounding region. It is the largest fledgling democracy in sub-Saharan Africa, and a failure of Nigerian democracy could plunge the West Africa subregion into a new round of political instability, economic uncertainty, and security problems, as was evident during the previous decade. A strengthened and more stable Nigerian democracy could have a stabilizing effect in West Africa, and important demonstrative effects throughout the continent.

Nigeria has more than 25 billion barrels of proven oil reserves. It provides abundant, and ever-larger volumes of sweet, light (environmentally attractive) crude oil to refineries on the U.S. eastern seaboard and accounts for 8 percent of U.S. national oil imports, and in the course of the Bush administration that figure will exceed 10 percent. U.S. direct foreign investment in Nigeria currently stands at $7 billion. By 2004, it could easily double.

Between half a million and a million Nigerians live in the United States, of whom 200,000 are American citizens. Their talent, wealth, and influence are now a part of America's political, cultural, and commercial life, and they remain tied in similarly diverse ways to Nigeria.

Nigerians figure prominently in transnational crime: especially narcotics, money laundering, and advance fee fraud. Between 35 and 40 percent of the heroin that enters the United States arrives through Nigerian syndicates and networks.

Nigeria is an activist middle power committed to leading developing-nation coalitions that press for greater debt relief, more favorable trade terms and macroeconomic conditionalities, enlargement of the UN Security Council, affordable access to medications for HIV/AIDS and other illnesses, and more generous external support in building elementary health infrastructure.

Finally, given the trajectory and magnitude of HIV/AIDS in Nigeria, the United States has little choice but to make Nigeria a high global priority in shaping effective strategies to reduce infection rates and deliver care and treatment to those persons living with HIV.

Under General Sani Abacha (1993–1998), Nigeria was on an exceedingly dangerous trajectory—threatening to itself, its neighborhood, international norms, and transnational security. Thankfully it reversed itself following Abacha's demise and entered the present democratic transition. From 1999 to the present, through historic luck, the courage of Nigerian leaders, and the popular will of the Nigerian people, hope and relative stability were restored in Nigeria and the most acute risks of catastrophe subsided. External parties, most notably the United States, played an essential role, both in pressuring and isolating Abacha and later in supporting the transition back to democracy.

Today, however, despite substantial recent gains, Nigeria is adrift. Chronically corrosive practices have not yet changed fundamentally: deep corruption and weak institutions persist, and Nigeria has yet to achieve enduring progress in macroeconomic management, policing, social services, and power and communications. National leadership has been weak in resolution of domestic interregional and interethnic tensions, and in moving the nation forward with respect to HIV/AIDS. If Nigeria continues to founder, it will be at increased risk of relapse into instability.

The core challenge that Nigeria's roller-coaster inheritance presents the Bush administration is to help reinvigorate and advance Nigeria's fragile democratic transition, ensure that Nigeria does not experience another precipitous breakdown, and strengthen collaborations in regional security, crisis diplomacy, HIV/AIDS, debt relief, governance reform, and domestic conflict resolution. Much hard work—broad, consistent engagement across several policy areas—is required to advance U.S. interests in Africa, but it will result in no quick breakthroughs. The Bush administration is fortunate to inherit a relatively sound bilateral relationship built upon much reciprocal good will. U.S. engagement in Nigeria for the past two years has been sustained at a high level, backed by a dynamic multisectoral assistance program of more than $100 million per year. The trick for the United States will be maintaining a disciplined focus upon its select priorities—with conviction, continued adequate resources, and sustained high-level backing—while navigating the setbacks and frustrations that are part of the Nigerian condition.

Nigeria's Recent Chapters: Near-Crash, Sudden Reversal, Mixed Recovery, Uncertain Drift

From 1993, when General Abacha assumed power, through his sudden death in June 1998, blunt repression, erratic rule, and unbridled plunder by the military regime pushed Nigeria to the brink of collapse. Thereafter, a transitional regime under General Abdulsalami Abubakar delivered on its promise to return Nigeria to democratic rule, and in June 1999 a newly elected president, Olusegun Obasanjo, took office. Thus far, Obasanjo's tenure has brought several important gains.

Democratic rule has ushered in a dramatic change in the human rights climate, the setting for political liberties, and the nature of civil-military relations. Hundreds of senior military officers have returned to civilian life, the rank and file have been downsized significantly, and plans are in place to modernize the armed forces. A tribunal has begun to redress extreme past violations of human rights. At the same time, Nigeria's internal climate has become far more tolerant of diverse opinion and independent civic organizations and is now rid of the paralyzing fear of the Abacha era.

Nigeria's economy has restabilized, and the government has passed anticorruption legislation, committed overtly to pursue privatization beginning with the telecommunications sector, and recruited into its ranks several reform-minded, promising new young leaders. Relations with the International Monetary Fund (IMF) and World Bank have been renewed, inflation stands at modest levels, and the government has until recently adhered to a policy of monetary restraint. Obasanjo has openly committed to reconciling with the deeply unstable, oil-rich Niger Delta, won passage of legislation to establish the Niger Delta Development Commission, and put into law a new formula by which the delta is to derive 13 percent of oil earnings.

Obasanjo has publicly exhorted the nation to mobilize against HIV/AIDS and pledged his government will pursue an aggressive action plan.

Through Obasanjo's determined efforts, Nigeria's continental leadership has been revitalized as well. Nigeria hosted the April 2001 Organization of African Unity (OAU) summit on AIDS in Abuja, and President Obasanjo, together with UN secretary general Kofi Annan, was on hand at the White House when President Bush announced that the United States would contribute $200 million to the Global Fund on HIV/AIDS. Nigeria has been an important advocate for debt relief and economic reform and revitalization, and, in concert with Presidents Thabo Mbeki of South Africa and Bouteflika of Algeria, President Obasanjo has spearheaded the Millennium African Renaissance Program (MAP). Finally, Nigeria is a continental leader in conflict resolution and has intervened as a force for peace—notably, in Sierra Leone, Côte d'Ivoire, Zimbabwe, and most recently in Sudan.

Nonetheless, the first two years of renewed democratic rule in Nigeria have also exposed profound obstacles, enduring high risks, and the limits of presidential leadership. Although no longer in immediate, acute danger of breakdown, Nigeria is a country adrift.

The president's office has done little to curb endemic corruption or create an environment conducive to foreign investment, and macroeconomic stability has stemmed little from policy and more from high world oil prices. The recent oil price dividend triggered a splurge of spending; the president's office demonstrated little capacity to withstand pressures from parliament, the state, and party insiders. After years of worsening immiserization, most citizens have yet to see the democratic turnaround translate into increased employment and incomes, enlarged economic opportunities, improved social services or reduced vulnerability to ramshackle, predatory institutions. External and domestic investment remains flat, except for select energy projects. Fuel shortages and power outages are no less common today than three years ago. The absence of genuine, structural economic reform means that Nigeria has made no progress in convincing external creditors to lighten its $32 billion debt overhang.

The president's office often also lacks control and coherence in relations with parliament (frequently deadlocked), Nigeria's 36 states, and military commanders. There has been no apparent will at the center to initiate a national constitutional dialogue on federal interstate relations that might mitigate north-south and Muslim-Christian cleavages, among other divisions. Instead, what has been seen are sudden shocks of escalating interethnic and interregional violence (for example, the upheavals in Kaduna in February and May 2000 that left 2,000 dead), along with actions by 10 northern state governors to embrace shari'a law, in apparent defiance of the center. Populist governors, likely linked with former northern military commanders and political leaders now bereft of national power, have consciously played upon the popular yearning for a moral code and dissatisfaction with national leaders' and national institutions' performance.

Nigeria's downscaled military is demoralized, its reinvention (and that of the national police) proceeds glacially, and it bears the stain of having violently razed the delta town of Odi, in November 1999, killing hundreds in retaliation for the deaths of a dozen policemen.

On HIV/AIDS, Nigeria is still far from implementing a national plan of action that will change high-risk behavior, lower infection rates, and begin to provide treatment and care to those ill from the virus. Also the country's health infrastructure has visibly deteriorated in the past decade, and its disease surveillance capacities are feeble and unreliable. Soon, if infection rates rise precipitously, mirroring the pattern in southern and eastern Africa, Nigeria will quickly be home to the world's largest population living with HIV. Indeed, Nigeria may already occupy that position—if adult prevalence rates exceed 5 percent, as many experts today believe. What might this mean? It is quite possible that Nigeria could attain 10–15 percent adult prevalence rates during the Bush administration's tenure and become one of Africa's—and the world's—greatest immediate HIV/AIDS challenges.

Obasanjo had hoped, and actively campaigned for, a disengagement from peacekeeping obligations in Sierra Leone, because of their high human and financial costs and their unpopularity at home. (Since entering Liberia as part of the ECOMOG West African force in 1990, Nigeria has expended more than $5 billion on peacekeeping and lost more than 2,000 soldiers. No other state worldwide made that level of commitment, and paid that high a price, toward peacekeeping.) That hope was soon thwarted, owing to the UN's inability to mount an effective peacekeeping operation in Sierra Leone and the RUF insurgency's capacity, backed by Liberia's President Charles Taylor, to foment instability and resist outside entreaties to abide by the July 1999 Lomé peace accord. Inexorably, Nigeria has found itself pulled back into Sierra Leone's and, by extension, West Africa's increasingly regionalized war that pits armies and militias from Liberia, Sierra Leone, and Guinea against one another. In effect, Nigeria has discovered, again, that it cannot separate itself from the deteriorating security of its neighborhood.

Obasanjo's domestic political base, an odd coalition assembled in haste in the run-up to the February 1999 national elections, has shrunk considerably. Obasanjo's ostensible political party, the People's Democratic Party (PDP), is an expedient assemblage of elites and veteran politicians, with little programmatic identity and sparse popular roots. As 2003 approaches, the PDP will reflate itself, no doubt, but how effectively, with what leadership, and against what competition remains unclear. Based on precedent, the incumbent leadership can be expected to use its control over the state to amass the PDP's electoral war chest. Indeed, the campaign has already begun.

In aggregate, these trends suggest that the lead-up to the 2003 elections carries a high potential for intrigue, shifting party alliances, electoral violence, and fraud. (The 1999 elections involved an estimated 9 million fraudulent or dubious votes out of a total of 29 million votes cast.) Citizens will assess their personal circumstances, their political allegiances, and the state of the nation, with an eye on bread-and-butter economic performance, the delivery of basic services, the levels of crime and social violence, the security of personal identity and religious expression, the effectiveness of presidential leadership, the performance of the political elite, the efficacy of efforts to address the HIV/AIDS challenge, and the implications of Nigeria's evolving regional security obligations. Nigeria's leaders will look outward to the United States and others to test the external world's seriousness in addressing debt relief, investment in elementary health care infrastructure, and preventive action in Zimbabwe and elsewhere.

U.S. Policy Trends

U.S. policy toward Nigeria is consistently dominated by three core elements: bilateral economic affairs (trade, investment, and energy); regional security (peacekeeping through ECOMOG); and governance (curbing corruption, promotion of democratic values and human rights, and strengthening democratic institutions). The central challenge to U.S. policymakers is mediating the inevitable tensions among them to forge an integrated and coherent approach.

U.S. relations with Nigeria were relatively normal up to mid-1993. Relations deteriorated steadily following the nullification of the June 1993 national elections (that would have brought Masood Abiola into the presidency), the ascendance to power of General Abacha, and subsequent sweeping state repression and wholesale plundering of state coffers by the Abacha regime. The United States responded with visa sanctions that denied high government officials and their family members the opportunity to travel to the United States. Direct flights between the United States and Nigeria ceased, owing to inadequate airport security, and the United States denied Nigeria annual certification for cooperation in antinarcotic efforts.

In the 1994–1996 period, Special Envoy Donald McHenry traveled eight times to Nigeria to seek moderation of the Abacha regime's practices. (Other special envoys separately engaged Nigeria on crisis management issues in Liberia and Sierra Leone.) U.S. bilateral assistance remained at very modest levels (approximately $6 million a year) focused on humanitarian aims. Two successive events significantly shifted discourse in Washington—the hanging of the Ogoni poet and leader Ken Saro-Wiwa and eight Ogoni environmental and human rights activists in November 1995 and the murder of Masood Abiola's wife in June 1996. In response, the United States stepped up its public condemnation of the regime and began an internal review of trade sanctions that examined the possibility of a freeze on assets, bans on new investment and provision of U.S. oil services, and divestment. Nonetheless, as fears mounted in 1996 to 1998 that Nigeria was sliding inexorably toward a violent breakdown that would destabilize the entire region, Washington remained internally divided and effectively deadlocked on additional punitive measures. In 1997, the United States quietly presented Nigeria a road map outlining quid pro quo reciprocal actions that could have walked Nigeria back from the brink and eased bilateral tensions. Abacha summarily dismissed this overture.

Two sudden deaths in mid-1998 radically altered Nigeria's internal politics and the context for U.S. policy: General Abacha died under mysterious circumstances in early June, and one month later Masood Abiola died of a heart attack. As General Abubakar carried forward transitional plans for a return to democratic rule, culminating in national elections in February 1999 and inauguration of a new president at the end of May, the United States responded swiftly.

High-level sustained leadership in Washington drove a dramatic turnaround in U.S. policy in 1999–2000. It began with U.S. secretary of state Madeleine Albright's designation in early 1999 of Nigeria as one of four global democratic transition priorities (along with Ukraine, Indonesia, and Colombia). During the course of the next 20 months, seven cabinet secretaries visited Nigeria, along with multiple senior subcabinet officers. President Obasanjo ventured to Washington in October 1999, and President Clinton reciprocated with a visit to Nigeria in August 2000. In November 1999, the United States and Nigeria launched in Washington the Joint Economic Partnership Commission (JEPC), a high-level mechanism intended to carry forward a bilateral dialogue on economic reform, debt relief, and corruption.

Bilateral assistance quadrupled to the present annual level of $107 million: concentrated on economic reform and anticorruption; HIV/AIDS and other infectious diseases; education; democracy-strengthening activities; and civil-military relations and restructuring of the military. At the end of 1999, direct airlinks resumed after improvements to airport security in Nigeria. In 1999 and 2000, Nigeria failed to meet the specific technical performance standards on counternarcotics and received two successive annual national interest waivers. In early 2001, the United States certified Nigeria's counternarcotics performance on the basis of several extraditions of indicted suspects to the United States.

As part of a $92 million U.S. program to enhance West African regional peacekeeping capacities for use in Sierra Leone, the United States committed in August 2000 to train and equip up to five Nigerian battalions (out of a maximum seven for the entire region) by the end of 2001. Both the U.S. and the Nigerian administrations appear ready to carry this initiative forward.

Nigeria entered a one-year IMF standby agreement in August 2000, subject to renewal. At the subsequent Paris Club meeting in December, the United States agreed to a "good will clause" that, if substantial progress were achieved in economic reform and meeting IMF targets, the United States would consider future debt rescheduling.

Recommendations

■ *Restore U.S. diplomatic capacities in Nigeria and Washington.* As a first priority, the new administration should staff and strengthen the U.S. embassy in Abuja, significantly expand diplomatic coverage in critical areas outside Abuja and Lagos, and fill its staffing requirements in Washington. Nigeria should be among the designated priority countries in the State Department's pilot special incentive program to attract young and mid-rank Foreign Service talent. Until Washington takes these steps, its ability to assist Nigeria in navigating the shoals of ethnic strife, economic reform, and civil-military tension will be severely limited.

■ *Lead a high-level, multilateral dialogue with Nigeria on debt relief, poverty reduction, and corruption.* The new administration should heed the warning by the Nigerian government, economist Jeffrey Sachs, and others that debt relief in Nigeria is a sine qua non of economic recovery and development. Cancellation of Nigeria's debt has become the rallying cry of the Obasanjo government, and the U.S.-Nigeria partnership will not move forward unless U.S. policymakers engage this issue in a forthright and meaningful way. But that engagement must emphasize using debt relief to leverage real reform, and fortify President Obasanjo's leverage against those within Nigeria who oppose reform. Given the wastage of the recent oil price dividend and the scant progress in privatization and anticorruption efforts, it is imperative that U.S.-supported debt relief be tied reliably to concrete achievement and that U.S. policy move forward in close concert with other G-8 member states and the EU. The United States should delineate achievable benchmarks in improved economic management, effective functioning of the Anti-Corruption Commission, and increased budgetary allocations toward school construction, water, electricity, and health infrastructure.

■ *Sustain a high-level bilateral dialogue.* The new administration should construct a forum for regular high-level dialogue with the Nigerian government. Options include a reformulation of the existing U.S.-Nigeria Joint Economic Partnership Commission, something modeled after the U.S.–South Africa Binational Commission, a subgroup on debt relief within the G7/G8, or an international contact group. Whatever the framework, systematic high-level dialogue should commence in 2001. Included within it should be high-level advice on how the presidency can better mobilize support and advance its strategic priorities through a forbidding political environment. That initiative might also involve the participation of private entities such as the Council on Foreign Relations or the U.S. Institute of Peace.

■ *Put the emergent security partnership on a sustained basis.* The new administration early on should engage in high-level consultations with the Nigerian government to determine how best to support Nigeria's peacekeeping role within ECOMOG and the United Nations. The recent initiative to train and equip peacekeeping battalions trained two Nigerian battalions that were deployed to Sierra Leone in early 2001 and have demonstrated improved performance. This initiative, however, has met with significant resistance by Nigerians, who criticize the program's conditionalities, elementary curriculum, and resource levels. Developments in Liberia and Sierra Leone attest to the important role that only the Nigerian military is capable of playing within the West African regional context. The administration should strive to resolve these differences quickly and win agreement—internally, with Nigeria, and with the U.S. Congress—on a program of sustainment for the next several years.

■ *Make collaboration on HIV/AIDS a priority.* The new administration should sharply expand its partnership with the Nigerian government to combat HIV/AIDS. Assistance levels, now approximately $20 million per year, are an important beginning but hardly commensurate with requirements. The administration should add $40 million per year immediately toward HIV/AIDS programs, add professional staff to the USAID mission, and launch an initiative to mobilize a concerted U.S., EU, UN, G-8, and corporate response.

■ *Enlarge contacts across the political spectrum to prepare for Nigeria's next elections.* The United States should begin early on to plan for and invest in Nigeria's next elections. Such an effort to ensure that electoral legitimacy is sustained and improved requires a continued high commitment of resources and ongoing engagement with Nigerian leaders, governing institutions, and civil society. The new administration should advocate sustained funding for Nigerian and African-based organizations that were involved in election training and monitoring and support U.S. nongovernmental involvement. USAID's Office of Transition Initiatives' work in Nigeria should be extended and its work on police reform enlarged. USAID should work to coordinate public and private efforts to strengthen civic institutions, nongovernmental capacity, community and media organizations, civilian-military relations, and police reform. The U.S. aid program should also provide support to the growing number of young Nigerian entrepreneurs and business managers who strive for higher business standards and closer global integration.

SOUTH AFRICA

South Africa matters significantly to U.S. national interests. As an "anchor" state in the southern African region, it wields enormous political clout, possesses one of Africa's most competent militaries, and is the economic linchpin of the Southern African Development Community (SADC). As the Bush administration seeks to consolidate its efforts in Africa, it will look to South Africa to play an ever-larger strategic role. And in recent years, South Africa has sought to extend its influence beyond southern African regional concerns and define itself as a interlocutor between the world's wealthy and poor states. Under the leadership of President Thabo Mbeki, the government has become increasingly active in international organizations and fora as an advocate for resource transfer from the developed to the developing world—most notably in the form of debt relief, access to pharmaceuticals, and more favorable international trade agreements.

South Africa's political transformation in the last 10 years serves as an example and an inspiration to civil rights and pro-democracy forces the world over. Yet the success of its democratic transition is not yet assured. Profound economic strains and the devastating impact of the AIDS pandemic—of which South Africa is the epicenter—will likely exacerbate political tensions in the coming years and sorely test the government's commitment to democracy.

South Africa presents the Bush administration with some major challenges: maintaining multiracial democratic processes within the country as the socioeconomic situation continues to change, coordinating policy if major crises develop in Zimbabwe or elsewhere that threaten the potential economic growth of the region, achieving greater consensus and mutual understanding on the AIDS situation, and forging a more successful economic partnership to overcome the sluggish growth that could threaten stability. Despite the continuing aid program, it is doubtful that the United States is providing resources equal to addressing these challenges.

The success of South Africa's constitutional development, its commitment to human rights and the rule of law, and its well developed civil society should not lead us to take it for granted. The transformation to long-term growth and stability in South Africa is far from over, and far from assured. If the country was worth 20 years of U.S. commitment, prior to 1994, it is worth more than the present commitment during the next decade. South Africa is a lesson in the long-term commitment that must be made to transitional societies. And if such countries are as important as South Africa is to many facets of U.S. foreign policy, then like Nigeria and Indonesia, the United States must find a way to sustain the level of commitment, resources, and attention that their development will require.

The Clinton Administration's Record

The Clinton administration played a significant role in facilitating the final stages of South Africa's transition from apartheid to democracy, concentrating high-level attention and resources in support of the transition process throughout the 1990s.

As it began, the Clinton administration benefited from several factors. The issues that had so divided the U.S. public and executive-congressional relations over southern Africa policy in the 1980s—sanctions, "constructive engagement," disinvestment, communist influence in the African National Congress (ANC), etc.—had all disappeared by 1993. The Bush administration had accepted and faithfully administered the sanctions policy and had reached out to the ANC. Namibia was independent and Cuban troops had withdrawn from Angola, achieving the objectives of constructive engagement. The Cold War had ended and with it much of conservative America's preoccupation with communist influence within the ANC. In South Africa a genuine reform movement was under way under President de Klerk. Nelson Mandela had left prison and made an enormously successful visit to the United States. Finally, the administration had a level of aid resources at its disposal—$80 million annually—that it could deploy to maximum effect.

The administration benefited from two other factors. There had been more than a decade of private as well as government support for South African professional and political development. The Ford and Rockefeller Foundations had invested in the advancement of legal and constitutional expertise among exiles and supporters of democracy in South Africa. Meetings between white South Africans and ANC leaders, forbidden in South Africa, had taken place in the confines of foundation seminars and events. Congress had initiated a scholarship program for black South Africans that had over time built a large cadre of expertise both within and outside South Africa that would lend itself to the transition process. Second, there was a high level of public attention to South Africa, built up through the symbiotic relationship fostered between the antiapartheid and civil rights movements and kept alive through churches, nongovernmental organizations, and state and local level governments. All of this facilitated the administration's ability to concentrate attention and resources on the situation.

Finally, the administration came to office just as the United Kingdom's role in South Africa was beginning to recede. Thus the United States became the major outside player in South Africa at a very critical time. The transition proved more difficult and time-consuming than anticipated, but the Clinton administration met these challenges well. Characteristics of the U.S. approach included:

- *A unified policy.* Throughout 1992–1994, U.S. policy was unified and consistently applied. This policy included unwavering support for the process being led by F.W. de Klerk and Nelson Mandela, and a recognition that other parties, including Inkatha, would have to play a lesser role than they demanded. It included the steady application of incentives to the process while holding back the final lifting of sanctions until there was political agreement from the ANC to lift them. And it concentrated resources on the peace process, education, and eventually support for the electoral process in a highly flexible and innovative manner. Congressional delegations reinforced and supported these policies.

- *High-level support from the United States.* Tremendous high-level attention was given to encourage South Africans in this process. The White House sent a large and extremely prestigious delegation to the funeral of ANC leader Oliver Tambo in early 1993, headed by Secretary of Health and Human Services Donna Shalala. This helped cement the confidence Mandela and other ANC leaders would have in the direction of U.S. policy. President Clinton met with both de Klerk and Mandela at the White House in the summer of 1993 and accompanied them to Philadelphia where both were to receive the Liberty Medal. Congress and the administration collaborated on new legislation in late 1993 that permitted more flexible use of aid resources to support the transition and that ended all remaining federal sanctions. Secretary of Commerce Ron Brown made a morale-boosting visit to South Africa shortly afterward to provide promises of economic support to a democratic South Africa and ahead of the election initiated several commercial programs. Brown would come back on several more occasions—always warmly received by the white community as well as the black majority. Numerous congressional delegations provided the same message of encouragement.

- *Delegation of authority.* The Clinton administration supported the assignment of a large and talented field mission and did not try to micromanage policy implementation. The embassy had the benefit of a sizable political staff, including Afrikaans and Xhosa language officers, and three consulates, enabling it to be in touch with the whole range of the political and social spectrum. On coming to office, the administration resisted political pressure to immediately replace the ambassador with a political appointee, whose delayed arrival and orientation during the critical first months of 1993 would have seriously interrupted and impeded the application of U.S. influence. There were no separate or surprise initiatives from Washington, rather full and complete communication and consultation on new ideas and proposals.

■ *An active public and private diplomacy to build credibility and use influence.* A mixture of public and private diplomacy was used both to convey U.S. positions and to cultivate credibility. The administration built up credibility with the principal actors—the ANC and the South African government—that permitted it to reach out to recalcitrant fringe parties without engendering suspicion. Every move made with the "homeland" leaders, with Buthelezi and with right-wing leader Constand Viljoen, was made with the knowledge of, and often the encouragement of, Mandela and elements of the South African government. The United States also used its public diplomacy to prod support from the South African business community and the media for the transition process and to take firm positions on violence from the right and left. It won the trust of leading right-wing figure Viljoen with high-level attention given him from the embassy, congressional delegations, and the Defense Department and appeals to his patriotism. From that position of credibility, the embassy was able to facilitate at a critical moment an agreement between his party and the ANC that led him to participate in the elections. The United States demonstrated in a public way that Buthelezi lacked both foreign support and the backing of the South African business community, all of which contributed to his decision, in the end, to join in the election and thus avert the specter of civil war.

■ *Respect for—and insistence on—South African responsibility.* The transition process was in the hands of the South Africans—at their insistence. The United States in turn held them to their responsibility, taking them to task when they faltered, staying back rather than trying to take over the process, but providing all the expertise and other forms of facilitative assistance possible. For example, the United States refused entreaties to officially "mediate" between Buthelezi and Mandela and persuaded other governments to do the same. Most important, the United States resisted calls from within South Africa to employ UN peacekeepers to quell the violence that plagued parts of the country during this time. Introducing an external force would have taken away the responsibility of the main parties to contain the violence, alienated the South African military, whose cooperation was crucial to the success of the transition, and been ineffective given the complexity of the underlying factors at work in the violence. On the other hand, the United States supported and helped the UN, EU, and OAU unarmed peace observers whose presence was extremely valuable.

■ *Flexible and imaginative use of resources to support civil society.* Largely left to its own devices, USAID found innovative ways to shift more support to black-led NGOs, who otherwise lacked the infrastructure to manage U.S. funds. It worked closely with the embassy and U.S. Information Agency (USIA) to identify important NGOs and individuals for such support and drew on a talented staff of both U.S. and South African employees with outreach in the community. In a highly unusual move, USAID transferred $1 million a year to USIA to utilize the latter's greater flexibility in responding to short-term opportunities to provide expertise to the negotiators and send observer teams to the United States.

After the 1994 election, the Clinton administration moved quickly to establish a Binational Commission (BNC) under Vice President Al Gore and Deputy President Mbeki. The BNC succeeded in developing ties between a wide spectrum of U.S. government departments and their South African counterparts and provided the opportunity to resolve difficult issues at the highest level. Through this mechanism, the long-contentious issue of prosecuting South African arms embargo violators was finally settled. Through the high-level contacts facilitated by the BNC, the United States persuaded South Africa to throw its weight and considerable influence behind an indefinite extension of the Non-Proliferation Treaty, one of the Clinton administration's highest foreign policy objectives. The administration did not welcome Mandela's involvement with Libya to accept the offer of a trial of suspected Libyan terrorists in the Netherlands, but Mandela probably did help resolve this issue in the U.S. favor. Despite various policy and other differences, Mandela and Clinton retained a close personal relationship and mutual respect that was evident during Clinton's visit to South Africa in 1998.

Nevertheless, the degree of partnership envisioned between the two countries in the wake of the 1994 election did not develop. Despite efforts by the embassy to dampen expectations, the large amount of attention to the transition gave rise to exaggerated expectations of U.S. aid to the new South Africa. Mandela surely expected South Africa to be a second Israel. When President Clinton announced a three-year $660 million program of support—actually quite a feat in an era of tight foreign aid—Mandela was shocked and several times in the ensuing years referred to the U.S. contribution as "peanuts." Nor did U.S. investment meet South African expectations, even though the United States emerged as the largest foreign investor. Finally, bitter trade disputes, especially the heavy punitive fines leveled on South African steel exports to the United States, revived latent anti-American feelings within South African circles. Overall, South Africa has, despite sound economic policies, failed to achieve growth rates of more than 2 percent annually since 1994, leaving unemployment at levels of 30 percent to 40 percent and leading to growing frustration within the country.

Cooperation on foreign policy issues also failed to meet expectations. South Africa was itself ambivalent about its foreign policy role, at once seeing itself as a major player but reluctant to throw its weight around or take too much attention away from domestic matters. When the United States in 1998 initiated the idea of an African Crisis Response Force, South Africa along with several other African countries was suspicious of U.S. motives and to this day has declined to participate in the revised African Crisis Response Initiative. Sharp divisions within SADC over the response to the crisis in the Democratic Republic of Congo (DRC), with Zimbabwe leading three SADC members into armed defense of the DRC government against Mandela's wishes, reduced South Africa's influence significantly. Meanwhile, the United States was perceived as being partial to the invading countries of Uganda and Rwanda, limiting the administration's ability to develop common ground either with South Africa or SADC in general. Little progress was made in finding common ground in responding to events in Zimbabwe either.

The Clinton administration had difficulty adjusting to the style and priorities of Mandela's successor, Thabo Mbeki. Mbeki badly botched his approach to the AIDS crisis, and South Africa's reputation as well, by immersing himself in the controversy over the relationship of HIV to AIDS. But Mbeki's principal and legitimate concern—that the AIDS crisis in Africa be seen in the context of the poverty, lack of health infrastructure, and added vulnerabilities arising from malnutrition—was not adequately picked up by the administration. Indeed, by initially defending the pharmaceutical industry's fight against South Africa's attempt to produce anti-AIDS drugs generically or import them more cheaply, the U.S. administration appeared insensitive to the seriousness of the nation's dilemma in fighting this disease. Those policies were subsequently reversed by the administration, but suspicion and differences in dealing with this major pandemic remain.

Nor did the administration capitalize on Mbeki's desire to be a principal intermediary between developing and developed countries on the issues of poverty and more equitable participation in the globalization process. The Clinton administration shared many of Mbeki's concerns—for example, debt relief, overcoming the digital divide, and better trade opportunities for developing countries. But problems with Congress and distractions elsewhere prevented the administration from forging a meaningful partnership with South Africa on these issues or advancing South Africa's role in this regard that is so important to Mbeki.

Finally, the Clinton administration failed to harness the support of the private sector in meeting South Africa's needs for investment.

Part of the problem rests with South Africa, which has not mounted anything like the effort required to compete in the United States with other countries in this arena. But some fault lies with the Clinton administration as well. Early in 2000 when Mbeki made a state visit, accompanied by 20 South African business representatives, the administration rolled out the red carpet, yet the guest list for the state dinner included scarcely any U.S. business representatives. Instead it was a reprise of the antiapartheid movement, emotionally satisfying but out of date with the pressing contemporary needs of the country.

Recommendations

- *Define a high-level mechanism to succeed the BNC.* The BNC at certain moments demonstrated its utility in managing contentious issues through timely interventions at upper levels. Early on, the Bush administration should seek agreement with South Africa on the mechanism to succeed the BNC and expedite its functioning. Otherwise there will be considerable risk of drift, unresolved wrangling at mid-levels, and missed opportunities.

- *Create a quiet, high-level dialogue on HIV/AIDS.* Improved engagement with the South African government on the HIV/AIDS crisis is required to reach consensus on a common strategy and move beyond mistrust and antagonism. Various factors—the decision by 39 multinational pharmaceutical corporations to withdraw their lawsuit against the South African government, the recent drop in prices of antiretroviral drugs, the White House announcement in May 2001 of a U.S. $200 million commitment to the global trust fund on infectious diseases, and new initiatives and increased collaboration within the UN and the G-8—create opportunities to engage South Africa anew on more focused and expansive collaborative efforts to combat AIDS.

- *Focus on stimulating economic growth.* The United States should intensify its dialogue with South Africa on promotion of U.S. private investment, trade, privatization, and international financial institutions. It should engage systematically, and at a high level, with U.S. corporate leaders and Congress to encourage greater private

sector activism and more favorable U.S. policies, including the for-
mulation of a new trade framework. South Africa's economic situation will remain critical during the next decade and central to
U.S. interests in the region. It is not certain that South Africa can
retain its commitment to the market-oriented policies it has pursued to date, or even its approach to multiracial democracy, if it
does not achieve greater growth and check unemployment. Brain
drain is stripping the country of needed skills across several technical areas, and overhauling the nation's education system to meet
those needs will take years. Attracting sufficient foreign investment will require a much better public campaign by the South African government and a more positive outlook for the free trade
zone within the region. Instability in Zimbabwe and the continuing war in Angola threaten the latter.

The United States should support African-led initiatives like the
Millennium Africa Renaissance Program developed by President
Mbeki, President Bouteflika of Algeria, and President Obasanjo of
Nigeria. This initiative seeks a new partnership to secure progress
on economic growth, private investment, and job generation in
stable political environments and promulgates a development
strategy to combat Africa's exclusion from the global economy.

■ *Expand U.S. assistance to support critical infrastructure.* The
Clinton administration sustained an annual assistance program
for South Africa of $50 million that fell far short of requirements,
particularly if compared with U.S. contributions toward other priority transitions such as Nigeria's. An annual program of $100
million, if not more, pledged during the next decade, would
strengthen U.S. contributions in crucial areas: education reform,
agriculture, the environment, and science. At the same time, the
United States should work to create an endowment for future cooperation so that U.S.–South Africa ties are less subject to the vi-
cissitudes of the foreign aid budget.

■ *Devise workable collaborations on the Zimbabwe crisis.* The Bush
administration faces a worsening crisis in Zimbabwe that will almost certainly have a major impact on South Africa and southern

Africa. A close working relationship with South Africa will be essential in shaping the international response, including coordinated efforts to contain violence, address the long-standing land issue, arrange a credible package of bilateral and multilateral incentives and disincentives, and enlist input from the United Nations, World Bank, and other SADC member states. During his visit to South Africa in May 2001, Secretary Powell, without South African complaint, publicly rebuked Mugabe and declared that it was time for Zimbabwe to move forward in the 2002 elections to a post-Mugabe future. This created a major new opening for collaboration and activism.

CHAPTER SIX

PURSUING U.S. ECONOMIC INTERESTS IN AFRICA
Peter M. Lewis

DESPITE PROFOUND ECONOMIC CHALLENGES IN AFRICA, the U.S. economic relationship with Africa has promise. The United States has a range of economic interests in the region, from oil and gas production to pharmaceuticals, telecommunications, and soft drinks. U.S. companies hold greater investments in Africa (more than $15 billion to date) than in either the Middle East or Eastern Europe, and U.S. total trade with Africa (about $20 billion annually) exceeds that with all the former communist states, including Russia. At least 15 percent of U.S. imported oil currently comes from Africa, and U.S. energy stakes there will approach strategic importance in the next few years as the United States seeks to diversify the sources of its energy supply.

At the same time, the region has receded to the margins of most global markets and is at risk of further marginalization. Africa faces a deep crisis of development. It struggles with slow economic growth, chronic poverty, and insurmountable debt. Thirty-three of the world's 41 poorest debtor countries are in Africa, and perhaps 220 million Africans (more than a third of the population) currently live on less than a dollar a day. There has been sporadic progress in recent years, but the region still faces enormous challenges in advancing economic reform, stimulating growth, improving governance, and making essential investments in people and critical infrastructure. These formidable difficulties are compounded by a heavy burden of external debt, declining world prices for most of Africa's exports, barriers to many global markets, and a shortage of investment and finance. In addition, the rising toll of AIDS could reduce the GDP of several countries by as much as a third over the next decade.

Rejuvenation of Africa's economies will require sustained, concerted attention from the international community, including sweeping debt relief, heightened development assistance, improved access to international markets, and better incentives for trade and investment. These steps will only produce results if linked to policy reforms and improvements in governance among the states of the region. U.S. leadership can be crucial in setting an agenda for reform and assistance, and marshaling resources to support Africa-led recovery. The Millennium Africa Renaissance Program, launched by Algeria, Nigeria, and South Africa, seeks a new partnership to secure progress on debt relief, private investment, and job generation in stable political environments. This Africa-led initiative warrants future U.S. support, if it can be translated into a concrete, viable program of action.

Whether Africa achieves greater stability and developmental promise, or whether it will be a locus of conflict, decline, and uncertainty, turns very much on the continent's economic fortunes. Continued economic stagnation and marginalization will almost certainly exacerbate political instability, conflict, and poverty, placing further demands on the United States for peacekeeping, humanitarian assistance, diplomatic intercession, and the alleviation of health crises. The persistence of corruption and weak institutions in these economies will also create further opportunities for transnational criminal activities, gray-market operations, and illicit migration, all of which will adversely affect U.S. interests. U.S. economic relations with Africa remain an important channel for furthering our regional and global U.S. interests.

The Clinton administration's economic policies toward Africa evolved through a series of ad hoc measures affecting trade and investment, debt, aid, and governance. The White House made efforts to encourage market relationships between the United States and Africa, with the intention of augmenting official resource flows and speeding the region's integration into the global economy. The administration recognized the profound resource constraints on development that external debt generates and declared its intention of alleviating some of the region's greatest financial burdens. U.S. agencies also devoted attention to the problem of governance, as reflected in efforts to reduce corruption, reform public administration, and encourage the rule of law.

During Clinton's second term, high-level visits to the continent by the president, the first lady, and senior cabinet officials focused greater public attention on Africa's problems and potential. Presidential leadership (embodied in the 1997 Partnership for African Growth and Opportunity) also spurred initiatives from other sections of government. A large, indeed unprecedented, assemblage of offices and senior staff were dedicated to African issues, spanning the treasury, commerce, energy, and transportation departments, as well as the U.S. Trade Representative's office and the Export-Import Bank.

The Clinton administration also supported more assertive steps toward debt relief, encouraging the multilateral Heavily Indebted Poor Countries (HIPC) Initiative through the International Monetary Fund (IMF), the World Bank, and the Paris Club, and calling for additional reductions in U.S. bilateral debt. The HIPC initiative has gained momentum recently, moving toward more rapid and comprehensive debt relief, along with provisions for directing resources to the alleviation of poverty in debtor countries. In the area of trade and investment, the African Growth and Opportunity Act, or AGOA, worked its way through Congress with presidential support. This bill provides for opening U.S. markets to African exports, improving incentives for U.S. investments, and encouraging better policies and governance to improve the setting for economic growth in Africa. Through a series of related measures, the Clinton administration increased the attention to economic links with Africa and sought additional public and private resources for infrastructure development in the region.

There has been, however, a large gap between aspiration and achievement in the domain of economic policy. Although many goals and initiatives during the Clinton years were commendable, they have so far produced few tangible results in terms of Africa's economic performance or the region's relationship with the United

States. There is scant evidence of more investment, increased trade, sufficient development assistance, or significant debt relief.

The disparity between the Clinton administration's aspirations and the actual achievements in the region may be attributed to a number of factors. The White House and Congress did not move in accord on African issues, and important measures such as trade promotion and debt relief languished without approval or funding. The United States did not adequately coordinate initiatives with major global partners (especially the G-7 and the European Union), slowing the fulfillment of important goals. Only at the close of President Clinton's second term did debt reduction measures appear to be gaining momentum, while AGOA will take effect only with time. This creates an opportunity for the Bush administration to strengthen U.S. leadership in this area.

Apart from these political concerns, there are further problems and challenges in the pursuit of U.S. economic interests in Africa. Economic advancement cannot occur in Africa without adequate resources. Debt relief is one important component of the funding picture, along with enhanced investment and trade, though these resources are at best prospective. Official development assistance is indispensable in providing support for African economies. Aid allotments, which have declined in the course of the Clinton years, should be increased to levels commensurate with U.S. goals in the region. Reform "on the cheap" will not yield results. A doubling of aggregate resource flows to Africa is justified on developmental grounds, and a growth of this magnitude could be achieved through a combination of increased aid, enhanced debt relief, multilateral resources, and private capital flows. Specifically, the Bush administration should seek to achieve a target of $5 billion in annual resources for Africa, including $1.5 billion in development assistance and other forms of direct aid, at least $2 billion in private direct investment, and $1.5 billion devoted to debt relief and HIV/AIDS.

If aid and other resource flows are to be effective, they must be guided by a strategy for addressing Africa's development needs. Economic revitalization requires much more than simply reforming macroeconomic policy or reducing the activities of intrusive governments. To achieve long-term growth, the states of the region must be able to make investments in social services, agricultural production, basic infrastructure, and targeted measures to alleviate poverty. In addition, African countries need better governance—more accountability, improved administration and technical capabilities, reduced corruption, greater public participation, and a stronger legal and regulatory environment—to provide a setting conducive to growth. Efforts by African governments to promote regional linkages and market integration will also play an important role in economic renewal. U.S. policies toward the region should therefore provide complementary resources for investing in Africa's people, and the capacities of governments to promote development. Collaboration between the public and private sectors—both here and in Africa—are essential components of an effective strategy for economic recovery.

A strategic focus also indicates the value of building selective partnerships with countries in the region. U.S. resources and efforts are most likely to yield results when concentrated in countries committed to better governance, reduced instability, and a reasonably consistent path of policy reform. In general, the most attractive partners in Africa will be governments that are democratizing, making social investments, seeking to alleviate conflict, and encouraging private sector development. These qualities may be weighted differently, of course, and particular cases may merit special attention, but U.S. commitments should follow a well-defined set of priorities and values rather than being driven by crises or bureaucratic lobbying. Selective partnerships do not imply a strict "triage" that will sever aid and investment for some countries while rewarding others. This approach does, however, imply a more discerning and careful allocation of assistance to favor countries that promise the best use of limited resources.

GENERAL RECOMMENDATIONS

- *Make an early and compelling public case on behalf of U.S. economic links to Africa.*

Africa is a significant economic partner, with linkages that may become strategic in the next few years. It is currently among the world's most active regions in terms of oil and gas development and may soon provide as much as a fifth of U.S. imported fuel. Trade and investment in the region have increased in the past decade, and substantial opportunities exist for further expansion. Recovery of the region's economies is obviously essential for Africans, but it will also benefit U.S. companies and markets. In addition, economic progress in Africa serves other prominent foreign policy goals, especially regional security and better governance.

■ *Build systematically on recent initiatives and the bipartisan support they enjoy in Congress.*

Congress, the White House, and the Bretton Woods institutions have introduced several promising measures that lay the groundwork for future policies toward the region. The current array of Africa-related offices in major U.S. departments and agencies offers the infrastructure for pursuing a more focused and effective economic agenda toward the region, and these facilities should be strengthened. The United States should fully fund its commitments to HIPC, support measures to widen and expedite the debt alleviation process, and take steps quickly to reduce U.S. bilateral obligations for poor debtor countries. The Bush administration should seek an expanded and more inclusive version of AGOA that will improve market access and investment incentives. In addition, enhanced government cooperation with the private sector can expedite the business activities of U.S. firms in Africa.

■ *Increase resource flows and deploy them strategically.*

The Bush administration should seek to double aggregate resource flows to Africa through increased aid, debt reduction, multilateral resources, and enhanced private capital flows. These resources should be directed toward the most promising targets of opportunity— through the use of selective partnerships with states that have demonstrated commitment to political and economic reform. A vigorous private sector response in Africa will require improvements in the ability of African governments to support a market system. Essential commitments to agriculture, social services, and infrastructure, as well as improvements in administration, all require adequate public resources. Stringent policy conditionality and admonitions for reducing the role of government, especially in the absence of sufficient funding, will not produce better economic performance in Africa.

■ *Assume a leadership role in coordinating domestic and multilateral policy responses.*

An integrated, coordinated approach by the United States and its international partners is clearly needed to address Africa's economic needs. U.S. policy must be consistent and prompt in such areas as foreign assistance, debt relief, and trade expansion. The administration can play a decisive role in setting an agenda and coordinating with Congress to enact and fund initiatives for African economic recovery. U.S. initiative and leadership can be crucial for an effective international response to Africa's developmental problems as well. It should act in concert with the G-7, the European Union, and multilateral financial institutions to provide debt relief, aid, global market access, and investment and policy assistance to beleaguered African economies. By venturing resources, working closely with economic partners, coordinating with the NGO community, and playing a prominent role in international organizations, the United States can leverage its wealth and authority to mobilize a response to Africa's economic needs.

DEBT

Africa is encumbered by an enormous debt burden. In 1996 sub-Saharan Africa's estimated external debt was $227 billion, representing more than the region's total gross domestic product and nearly three times the value of exports. As much as a fifth of Africa's annual export revenues go toward debt service. The debt overhang in Africa is among the most severe of any region in the world, and most countries are clearly unable to repay these liabilities. The resources devoted to servicing external debt diminish the funds needed for critical investments in education, health, and infrastructure. In short, debt represents a dead weight on African development and is one of the largest impediments to economic recovery in the region.

In recent years, the question of debt reduction has emerged as a central issue among G-7 governments, international institutions, and nongovernmental organizations (NGOs) concerned with African development. Debt relief has risen to the top of the policy agenda in U.S. economic relations with Africa, and bipartisan consensus about the importance of debt alleviation has increased markedly.

In contrast to Latin America and Asia, where private creditors are heavily involved, most African debt is owed to G-7 governments and the Bretton Woods institutions. This provides an opportunity for comprehensive debt relief, as creditors can more readily coordinate a program of debt reduction. From 1988 through 1996, a series of Paris Club proposals for poor countries focused on rescheduling external obligations, with some associated write-offs of bilateral debt. These programs were deemed insufficient for addressing the problem, especially as debt obligations continued to rise for low-income countries.

In 1996, prompted in part by the G-7, the Heavily Indebted Poor Countries Initiative was proposed by the IMF and the World Bank (international financial institutions, or IFIs) to provide sweeping debt reduction for low-income states. The Clinton administration provided encouragement, political backing, and financial pledges for HIPC.

The HIPC framework represents a new approach to debt relief for the poorest countries. The program includes multilateral debt, which had previously been ineligible for rescheduling or cancellation. By grouping multilateral and bilateral debt, this framework offers the opportunity for an inclusive workout of the main categories of official debt owed by African countries. It also focuses more centrally on reduction of debt stock, rather than simply rolling over or extending present commitments. Although previous Paris Club arrangements allowed for significant reductions in bilateral debt stock, very little actual relief had occurred prior to the introduction of HIPC. Furthermore, HIPC is targeted to the most needy states, many of which suffer the greatest debt overhang and the most acute financial constraints.

In line with preceding debt proposals, qualification under HIPC is linked to policy conditionality. Eligible countries are required to establish a track record of policy reform, and the initial HIPC program stipulated a six-year certification process leading to debt reduction.

The program emphasized a standard prescription of macroeconomic reform, including fiscal restraint and market liberalization. This orthodox stance was essentially a continuation of preceding Paris Club programs.

The HIPC framework, although welcomed as a constructive innovation, has also attracted substantial criticism from policy analysts, nongovernmental organizations focused on African debt and development, some members of Congress, and many commentators in the HIPC countries themselves. In particular, a large international coalition of NGOs, most prominently the Jubilee 2000 grouping, has pressed for debt cancellation and has been critical of the extent and pace of debt relief, as well as the conditions attached to such write-offs.

The most general objections call attention to the program's cumbersome procedures, which apply complex conditions and require a lengthy certification period before actual reductions are conferred. By 1999, only a handful of eligible HIPC countries were approaching the latter stages of the decision process. In addition, some analysts have urged a stronger focus on improving popular welfare in poor countries by ensuring that resources freed by debt relief are allocated to social spending and poverty alleviation efforts.

At a 1999 meeting in Cologne, the IFIs sought to address some of these objections by expediting the approval procedure for HIPC relief and explicitly including the establishment of poverty reduction programs in the eligibility requirements. The September 2000 IMF–World Bank meeting in Prague streamlined the approval process, pledged stronger financial backing for the program, and promised prompt reductions for a substantial number of eligible countries. Critics have continued to express concern about the burdensome requirements of new antipoverty stipulations, the insistence on orthodox policy reform, and the lagging progress on actual debt cancellation.

The Clinton administration urged debt relief for Africa and supported the HIPC initiative. The U.S. government unilaterally forgave a portion of bilateral debt owed by poor African countries, and since 1996 has worked through the HIPC framework. But a lack of accord between the White House and Congress has hindered the progress of debt relief. Congress has been slow to authorize the $600 million pledged as the U.S. contribution to the HIPC Trust Fund and delayed funding additional reductions of U.S. bilateral debt, or allowing the IMF to release a portion of its gold reserve sales to finance the program. The congressional authorization in October 2000 of some $435 million for the HIPC Trust Fund, and approval of the use of the IMF gold proceeds, was a step in the right direction. Previous delays have substantially impeded progress on HIPC and weakened U.S. leadership on this issue.

The HIPC initiative is currently the most viable channel for broad-based debt reduction in Africa, as it brings the Bretton Woods institutions and the G-7 countries together in a common forum with clearly designated procedures. The next administration will face a number of challenges in making HIPC work and thereby achieving the goal of furnishing greater resources for development in Africa. First, U.S. commitments to HIPC must be fully funded, which means paying the U.S. contribution to the HIPC Trust Fund and allowing IFIs to take appropriate steps to support the program.

In addition, the administration should consider further reductions of U.S. bilateral debt, in advance of reductions under HIPC. The current debt of African HIPC countries to the United States is about $5.4 billion, which constitutes 3.7 percent of African HIPC debt. The reduction of bilateral debt will be of modest cost to the United States, especially because much of this debt is unlikely to be paid anyway. Although such action will admittedly confer small resources to African debtors, unilateral action by the United States can signal U.S. commitment and enhance U.S. leadership on this issue.

The United States should also exercise greater flexibility on the issue of policy conditionality. There is no question that debt relief should be linked to the adoption of appropriate economic policies among debtor countries. Policy conditionality can be reviewed, however, to reduce the number and scope of conditions and to match conditions more appropriately to the capacities of governments in the region. Simpler conditionality would expedite certification under HIPC. In addition, agencies such as USAID could be engaged to assist debtor governments with the development of antipoverty programs to meet the qualifications of the initiative. The United States should also urge leeway in the IFIs' application of conditionality for countries in special circumstances—for example, those emerging from sustained conflicts or undergoing difficult political transitions. In this vein, it will also be advisable to add some "non-IDA only" countries such as Nigeria to the program.

Recommendations on debt relief

■ *Exercise leadership, at home and abroad, on debt reduction for Africa.*

Debt reduction must be among the highest priorities of U.S. policy toward Africa, because the region's economic prospects are linked to this important reform. The Bush administration and Congress must cooperate to fund existing commitments to the HIPC initiative, and funding should be expanded. Cancellation of most U.S. bilateral debt will require only modest resources from the United States and can enhance U.S. standing as an international leader on this issue. U.S. leadership is critical to realizing broad debt reduction and can be an important catalyst for action.

■ *Support faster and deeper debt relief through the HIPC initiative.*

The broad features of HIPC have merit. The program is multilateral, includes the most important categories of official debt, and is generally targeted to the most needy countries. Debt relief is contingent on better economic management by African governments and emphasizes measures to reduce poverty and increase social spending. HIPC should be expedited and modified—especially through a faster decision process, including simpler and more flexible conditionality—to provide speedier debt reduction to more countries and to deliver resources for development needs.

ENERGY

Africa is an important global source of petroleum, supplying approximately 7 percent of the world's supply. The United States is an ever-larger customer, with at least 15 percent of U.S. annual oil imports currently originating from the region. Proven reserves of oil and gas have increased significantly (from 59 billion barrels in 1990 to 75 billion barrels in 2000) as have estimated reserves. It is now predicted that Africa will provide one out of every four new barrels of oil to come on stream (outside the Gulf states) in the next four years. Traditional partners like Nigeria and Angola will increase their production, and emerging sources like Equatorial Guinea and Chad will become much more significant. For U.S.-based oil service companies, particularly in Louisiana, Texas, and California, these energy-rich African states account for more than 100,000 American jobs.

Africa's energy resources constitute important national interests for the United States, with the potential to become strategic in the next decade. U.S. reliance on African energy sources has grown during the past decade and will likely exceed 20 percent of U.S. energy imports during President Bush's tenure. Over the longer term, the decline of North Sea production expected over the next 10 years will heighten the significance of African output, as the United States seeks to limit its reliance on Middle Eastern sources.

Currently, U.S. direct investment in Africa's petroleum sector (about $10 billion) exceeds its stake in either Latin America, Eastern Europe and Central Asia (including all the states around the Caspian Sea), or the Middle East. Given the potential for Africa's energy development, U.S. firms have increased their commitment and over the next decade may invest as much as $50 billion in regional exploration and production. Furthermore, the potential of new energy activities, including natural gas production, liquefied natural gas, refining, petrochemicals, and electricity production, signal the possibilities for considerable market expansion.

A troubling feature of Africa's energy picture is the concentration of resources in countries that are undemocratic, politically unstable, or involved in large-scale conflict. Nigeria, Angola, Gabon, and Algeria are currently the region's largest exporters, while additional resources are on stream or in development in Cameroon, Sudan, Congo, Democratic Republic of Congo, Chad, and Equatorial Guinea. For many of these countries, oil has been, at best, a mixed blessing. The wealth garnered from energy exports might appear as a boon to development, but in practice much of it has been squandered or mismanaged. Too often leaders have commandeered revenues, interest groups (particularly the military) have competed for benefits, and the infusion of resources has served to incite or sustain conflict. For the residents of oil-producing localities, there is a special irony of deprivation in the midst of potential wealth. Many of these communities have experienced environmental degradation, economic neglect, political repression, and human rights abuse. Governments and firms both share responsibility for these problems.

The relationship between resource wealth, weak governance, and instability is complex, though there are policy interventions that can mitigate some of these negative effects, including fiscal reforms, decentralization, targeted anticorruption efforts, regulatory and legal changes, selective privatization of downstream petroleum activities and electricity production, and development initiatives for oil-producing communities. Reforms of this type will offer benefits to producing countries and a more hospitable environment for investors.

The development of the $3.7 billion Chad-Cameroon pipeline project, launched in late 2000, is perhaps the most innovative approach to these problems, enlisting cooperation among governments, multilateral donors, oil firms, and NGOs. In particular, the World Bank has played a leading role in creating arrangements for financial transparency and an autonomous development fund as the repository of project revenues. Despite the problems of implementing this model, it presents an important innovation in the way resources have been developed in Africa. The World Bank's current audit of Angola's energy sector is another significant step in attempting to curb mismanagement and the illicit use of funds.

U.S. companies confront a number of difficulties in Africa's energy sector. Although there are enormous opportunities, many operators find it difficult to attain a predictable or secure business climate. As major investors and revenue providers in the countries where they operate, these firms are unavoidably involved in the political and developmental problems of their hosts. They face problems of instituting reliable commercial arrangements with host governments, establishing good relations with local communities, and providing security for employees and facilities. In many instances, foreign firms are convenient targets for economic grievances or dissident action. They are also frequently entangled in a nexus of corruption.

The policies and business practices of private companies obviously influence their ability to negotiate these hazards. In recent years, several firms, chiefly in Nigeria, have been embroiled in local security problems and incidents of environmental damage. Local activists and international NGOs have criticized the major oil companies for lax environmental standards, human rights abuses, and collusion with repressive and corrupt leaders. These concerns affect the companies' reputation and competitive standing. Some of the larger international firms have shown initiative in trying to clarify best practices with regard to community relations, the environment, human rights, and corruption. These efforts have benefited from dialogue and engagement with local community representatives and international NGOs. The Department of State has also cooperated with U.S. firms in attempting to delineate corporate security procedures that are compatible with good community relations and human rights.

Apart from this targeted effort, the Department of Energy has undertaken a broader initiative to support U.S. interests in Africa's energy sector, including an analysis of the region's energy resources and the identification of investment and trade opportunities. The 1999 Tucson meeting of African energy ministers, U.S. officials, and business representatives provided a forum for discussing the development of the region's energy resources and the respective roles of the public and private sectors in this area. This gathering addressed the place of the energy sector in African economic development, the environmental issues related to activities in this sector, the general commercial climate in Africa, and the areas of reform that could promote investment, trade, and enhanced benefits for the countries of the region. In particular, the meeting highlighted reform of governance and macroeconomic management and the affirmation of principles of corporate citizenship.

These efforts, although ad hoc, have helped to trace the outlines of a coherent energy policy toward Africa. One shortcoming in the current efforts has been the lack of resources allotted to these agencies for their programs. Energy policy in Africa should not simply be seen as another improvised "add-on" to the many areas supported by USAID and other development funds. Improvements in the climate for investment, trade, economic management, and corporate citizenship are not merely defensive steps to protect existing interests. These reforms can help realize the considerable untapped potential of Africa's natural resources. A more secure, stable, and transparent environment will contribute to higher investment and greater revenues from the energy sector.

Recommendations on energy

■ *Articulate and fund a U.S. energy policy toward Africa.*

U.S. imports of oil and gas from Africa have increased substantially in the last decade—an upward trend that will continue, as will the reliance of U.S. jobs on an expanding African energy marketplace. As the United States seeks to diversify its sources of energy, the U.S. stake in the African oil and gas sector will deepen. U.S. policy toward the region should place a priority on energy trade and related issues. A coherent energy policy—which has been lacking in past administrations—will define U.S. interests in the region, set goals, and introduce programmatic measures to ensure stability of supply, a favorable business climate for U.S. firms, environmental preservation, and developmental benefits for African economies. The United States should engage other G-7 countries more regularly and effectively to cooperate on these policy goals.

■ *Create a better business environment through governance reforms.*

U.S. companies, although already substantially committed in Africa, will increase their involvement as new resources are discovered and market access to the region's energy sectors is extended. Reform of the political context in the resource sector offers benefits to African economies as well as foreign investors. Greater financial transparency, improved management, and enhanced technocratic capabilities can increase the contribution of resources to local development. A better setting for business, including reduced corruption, more transparent regulation, law and order, and improved public services, will also encourage investment and trade. The Bush administration can contribute to these through expanded technical support in creating regulatory regimes, accounting mechanisms, and other anticorruption measures.

■ *Encourage partnership with the private sector to ensure best practices.*

U.S. firms have legitimate interests in maintaining security of property and conducting business without arbitrary political interventions. At the same time, many companies have come under scrutiny for their community relations, environmental impact, and security practices. These concerns pose real liabilities for operations in the region. The U.S. government can play a constructive role in engaging with U.S. companies and nongovernmental organizations, along with governments and communities in the region, to achieve greater consensus on best practices and to address tensions arising from private sector activities.

TRADE AND INVESTMENT

Africa currently has substantial economic links to the United States, with enormous potential for growth and diversification. Most of Africa's exports are mineral or agricultural commodities, including petroleum, diamonds, platinum, gold, aluminum, titanium, coal, cocoa, coffee, cotton, timber, and fish. The region chiefly imports manufactured goods from Europe, although Africa is also an important consumer of U.S. wheat.

From the vantage of the United States, the transatlantic market relationship is proportionally small—about 1 percent of total U.S. exports, imports, and direct foreign investment is devoted to transactions with Africa. Overall, the United States imports about $15 billion worth of goods annually from the region, while Africa buys roughly $6 billion in U.S. exports. American firms invest $1 billion to $2 billion annually in sub-Saharan Africa. Trade with the region has risen over the last decade, from about $13 billion (exports and imports) in 1990 to a peak of $22.5 billion in 1997. Following a drop after the Asian economic crisis, trade has recovered to about $20 billion today. These exchanges are highly concentrated: 80 percent of

U.S. imports come from four countries (Nigeria, South Africa, Angola, and Gabon), while five states (South Africa, Nigeria, Angola, Ghana, and Kenya) account for 70 percent of African imports from the United States.

The trade and investment relationship can be quite significant for Africa's small markets and poor economies. In the last decade, worldwide official development assistance has remained virtually unchanged, while global private capital flows have increased fivefold. Regrettably, Africa has failed to benefit from the dramatic expansion of international trade and investment. Development aid to the region has declined on a per capita basis, while there has been virtually no increase in private capital and minimal growth in trade flows. The relative stagnation of trade and investment is contrary to the trend for nearly all other developing regions. In the past, Africa's trade has been hindered by low domestic incomes, small market size, deficient infrastructure, and adverse policies. Further integration of African economies into the world economy will provide substantial opportunities for economic growth.

In its early years, the Clinton administration put less emphasis on the U.S. market relationship with Africa. Upon conclusion of the Uruguay Round trade forum in 1994, the administration, urged by Congress, issued an annual report on U.S.-African trade relations and provided modest initiatives to encourage commerce with the region. In U.S. bilateral aid relations and through participation in the IFIs, policy conditionality encouraged governments to liberalize their trade regulations and promote private enterprise, but apart from these stipulations there was a limited scope of complementary measures from the U.S. side.

In 1997, the African Growth and Opportunity Act was introduced in Congress. The bill focused on improving trade with Africa by opening U.S. markets to Africa and by encouraging further reform to make African markets accessible to U.S. goods and investment. Nearly concurrent with the proposal of AGOA, the administration initiated the Partnership for Economic Growth and Opportunity in Africa, which included a series of complementary initiatives through the Generalized System of Preferences (GSP), the Office of the U.S.

Trade Representative (USTR), the Export-Import Bank, and the Overseas Private Investment Corporation (OPIC). The initiative also called for assistance to develop African infrastructure, in which the Department of Transportation has taken a leading role. Also during this period, the president and the first lady made trips to the region, highlighting successes and opportunities in Africa and seeking to spur the economic relationship. Presidential initiatives were accompanied by expansion of other Africa-related programs in the treasury, commerce, and energy departments.

In Congress, meanwhile, despite substantial bipartisan support for AGOA, the bill was criticized on the issue of competition in the textiles sector, as well as concerns about policy conditionality and debt relief. AGOA was eventually passed into law in May 2000. The passage of the bill signaled a change of emphasis in U.S. economic policy toward Africa, by seeking to increase the role of market linkages in the economic relationship with African countries. The language of the bill also addresses a prominent concern in the promotion of African trade—namely, the limited access of African countries to the markets of the industrialized North. In general, these are constructive policy directions.

Some concerns should be noted, however, regarding AGOA and U.S.-Africa trade policy in general. First, the legislative process has encumbered the final version of the trade bill with a number of qualifications and restraints that considerably narrow the benefits available to African countries. AGOA could turn out to be a largely symbolic measure unless criteria for eligibility (particularly regarding the range of products and the degree of market access) are widened. Another central feature of the bill is its insistence on economic policy reform as a criterion for eligibility. This may generally be appropriate, but there will be instances of countries emerging from deadly conflicts, or those struggling with democratic transitions, that may merit economic support even if they do not reflect an ideal policy mix. Conditionality should be treated flexibly in applying the bill.

African critics have said that AGOA signals a relative downgrading of aid in favor of private sector activities. This may not have been intentional, but it is true that the aid budget for Africa has declined incrementally in the past eight years, and the next administration must make efforts to reverse this trend. Trade and capital flows can be an important catalyst of growth, but they do not replace the official assistance needed for social spending, poverty reduction, improvements in agricultural production, the development of infrastructure, better policy design, or enhanced public administration. A firm partnership between the public and private sectors is required to fulfill the promise of U.S.-Africa economic relations and to promote effectively the revitalization of African economies.

The movement toward regional cooperation and market integration may serve to develop trade and investment flows. The administration should encourage, through bilateral and multilateral assistance, efforts by African governments to reduce regional economic barriers and to enhance linkages of infrastructure, finance, and information.

In recent years, the administration has established a number of Africa-related programs and regional offices. These measures should be continued and, if possible, expanded. In particular, there should be broader efforts to provide market information and advisory services to U.S. firms, as well as complementary trade promotion by U.S. representatives in Africa. Commercial representatives at U.S. embassies throughout Africa can play a role in this effort.

Recommendations on trade and investment

- *Build trade and investment relations with Africa, starting with the framework provided by AGOA.*

There is an unfulfilled potential for deeper economic links with Africa. Given the region's large, underdeveloped markets and abundant resources, the development of trade and investment can yield substantial mutual benefits. AGOA provides opportunities for improving African access to U.S. markets and enhancing opportunities for U.S. firms in Africa. The growth of economic interactions would offer considerable mutual benefits. The Bush administration should take assertive steps to promote market relations, including revision of the trade bill to expand its eligibility and activities.

■ *Expand complementary efforts to promote trade and investment.*

The Clinton administration's initiatives through the GSP, OPIC, Export-Import Bank, USTR, and departments such as treasury, commerce, transportation, and energy have strengthened U.S. knowledge and capacities to address African issues and provide effective policies. These efforts should be expanded and adequately funded. U.S. agencies and overseas commercial representatives can also provide more effective advice and assistance to U.S. firms considering business in Africa, as well as African companies seeking to enter U.S. markets.

■ *Provide additional assistance through aid and multilateral resources.*

Vigorous private sector activities require a supporting government role. Concerted partnership between the public and private sectors—on the part of the United States as well as African countries—is key to advancing investment and trade. Market incentives must be assisted by public investments in human capital, infrastructure, technology, and information flows. Enhanced development assistance and support through IFIs will be essential to realizing the potential contained in AGOA. Efforts by African governments to promote regional economic integration will also advance trade and investment, and regional integration efforts should be supported by multilateral and bilateral assistance.

FOREIGN ASSISTANCE

Foreign assistance has been among the most controversial elements of U.S. policy toward Africa. Total U.S. aid to Africa (including military assistance) peaked in 1985, at about $2.4 billion. This diminished quickly in the aftermath of the Cold War, with military assistance leading the reductions. Development assistance has also been trimmed in the course of the 1990s, and economic support funds (ESF—a flexible category of funds allotted to countries in special circumstances) have been modest and inconsistent. Total funds allocated to USAID for Africa in 1990 stood at about $1.1 billion, increasing to $1.9 billion in 1992, and diminishing steadily to $1.15 billion in 1999. The specific category of development assistance stood at $822 million in 1992 and diminished to $739 million in 1999. In essence, the past decade has brought no increase in economic assistance to Africa, and on a per capita basis, allocations have decreased substantially.

During the course of the Clinton administration, general levels of funding and the organizational position of USAID dominated the aid agenda for Africa. In the wake of the Cold War and the controversial intervention in Somalia, there was a widespread reevaluation of foreign aid. The 1994 elections produced a congressional majority critical of external commitments, particularly in Africa, where previous assistance had often yielded disappointing results. Supporters of aid to Africa, within the administration as well as in Congress, resisted the sharp cuts assayed by congressional opponents. Nonetheless, development assistance to Africa dropped by nearly a fifth in 1996, and ESF was virtually eliminated. These levels moved up incrementally in subsequent years, and ESF increased dramatically in 1999 (to $92 million), largely in response to the Nigerian transition. Still, net levels of development assistance to Africa dropped (by about 10 percent) during the Clinton years.

Present financial commitments are insufficient to support real advancement in African economies. African countries need resources for essential investments in education, the expansion of health services, agricultural research and extension, the development of basic infrastructure, and institutional reforms to improve administration and facilitate market transactions. Some of these funds will come from multilateral institutions and other donors, but U.S. development assistance can be an important source of support. Although there is understandable skepticism about the effectiveness of aid to Africa, the answer is not to cut funding but to improve the design and implementation of programs to provide greater value. U.S. assistance to Africa has been spread across too many categories and programs and has been filtered through a USAID Africa Bureau that is in disarray. More aid for Africa will be beneficial if it is better targeted and administered, and the Bush administration should work with Congress toward these goals.

The institutional standing of USAID has been another critical issue. Proposals to incorporate USAID into the Department of State were resisted by agency officials, and its organizational autonomy was preserved. Since April 1999, USAID has been placed formally under the secretary of state's authority, although it continues to operate independently. This affirmation of the status quo carries both advantages and liabilities. On the positive side, USAID's status as an independent, professional organization focused on the design and oversight of development assistance was preserved. On the other hand, USAID has been largely peripheral to the policy process regarding Africa, and development assistance has been isolated from other aspects of policy in the region. The Bush administration will need to address the status of USAID, balancing the need to ensure its coherence and professional autonomy with the importance of integrating its decisionmaking into broader U.S. foreign policy calculations.

Development assistance to Africa will be most effective if driven by a coherent strategy for the region that concentrates on the select goals of promoting economic growth, conflict prevention and stability, and health. USAID's current approach to African economies emphasizes a wide range of tasks and programs under the umbrella of sustainable development and governance reforms. USAID should identify a specialized role—focusing on a few core goals and areas of competence—that can be coordinated with other U.S. policy initiatives at the regional and country level. The United States should also seek better coordination with other G-7 countries, the IFIs, and international organizations. Some tasks and resources can be delegated to other donors, while USAID and related agencies concentrate their efforts.

Another measure that can help to improve the effectiveness of development assistance is to pursue selective partnerships with aid recipients. The United States should concentrate resources and programs on countries that are highly important to U.S. interests, that stabilize and strengthen their surrounding regions, that are committed to economic and political reform, and that have adequate absorptive capacity. The most attractive aid partners in the region will be those making progress on resolving conflict, improving governance, undertaking basic macroeconomic reforms, enhancing social conditions, and making institutional changes to improve aid performance. Aid selectivity might not always result in a rigid "triage," but it should guide the focus of resources on more auspicious partners.

Recommendations on U.S. foreign assistance

■ *Restore development assistance to appropriate levels.*

U.S. development assistance for Africa has diminished in the 1990s, and since 1992 overall appropriations for USAID (including all aid categories) have been nearly cut in half. Two of the most important brackets, development assistance and economic support funds, declined from $910 million in 1992 to $800 million in 2000—a steep drop, on a per capita basis, in funding for the region. Without adequate resources, the United States cannot play an effective role in fostering economic growth in Africa. Funds are needed for social spending, poverty alleviation, basic economic investments, and governance reform. Increased aid, if properly directed, can bring significant results. At minimum, allotments for development assistance and economic support funds should be targeted at $1 billion annually, in addition to resources for humanitarian relief, food aid, and multilateral programs.

■ *Coordinate aid more effectively with a broader strategy for Africa, and incorporate USAID as a participant in the policy process.*

U.S. aid activities have not been adequately guided by a general set of policy priorities for the region. Although USAID has articulated an approach to development, this is not always coordinated with central aspects of U.S. policy. USAID should retain its role as an autonomous, professional agency for development assistance, but this should be balanced with the incorporation of aid efforts into broader U.S. policy goals in the region. Coordination of U.S. development assistance with the efforts of other G-7 countries, the IFIs, and international organizations will also enhance aid effectiveness.

■ *Create selective partnerships to enhance aid effectiveness.*

There is no question that previous investments in aid to Africa have yielded disappointing results. Aid effectiveness can be enhanced by targeting assistance to countries more likely to pursue essential reforms in governance, social policy, economic programs, and security relations. More selective assistance can increase returns and also has the potential to encourage successes that will carry "demonstration effects" in the region.

CHAPTER SEVEN

STRENGTHENING U.S. GOVERNMENT HUMANITARIAN ACTION IN AFRICA
Victor Tanner and Nan Borton

DURING THE PAST 12 YEARS, humanitarian assistance to crisis zones worldwide has quadrupled. Total U.S. humanitarian outlays exceeded $1.5 billion in 1999. Whether as a component of wider multilateral humanitarian intervention, such as in Somalia, Bosnia, and Kosovo, or in largely neglected conflicts, like Afghanistan and Sudan, humanitarian assistance has been a significant—at times central—component of U.S. foreign policy. Nowhere is this truer than in Africa, where consistently one-half to two-thirds of U.S. humanitarian assistance has been destined.

The Bush administration signaled early on in its tenure its intention to scale back international commitments and shy away from humanitarian interventions in Africa and elsewhere. Most notably, Mr. Bush asserted in the second presidential debate with Vice President Al Gore that his predecessor "did the right thing" by taking no military action to prevent or halt the genocide in Rwanda in 1994. This resolve to avoid military interventions notwithstanding, the next four years will feature persistent humanitarian challenges—particularly in Africa—along with persistent domestic pressures to act. Humanitarian needs tied to Africa's continental crisis will remain huge, and the prospects for the next four years are forbidding. Thousands die every year in ongoing crises in the Democratic Republic of Congo, Sudan, Angola, Burundi, Sierra Leone, and now Guinea. Precipitous decline threatens important mid-level countries—Kenya, Zimbabwe, and Côte d'Ivoire. Drought in the Horn and floods in southern Africa are

U.S. Government Humanitarian Assistance

By law, the U.S. president can provide humanitarian assistance through several channels that are appropriated by Congress:

- U.S. Agency for International Development (USAID) through

    - the Office of U.S. Foreign Disaster Assistance (OFDA),

    - the Office of Transition Initiatives (OTI), and

    - Food for Peace (FFP), as well as

    - some disaster monies available to USAID missions and ambassadors

- U.S. Department of Agriculture (USDA) through its emergency food programs;

- U.S. State Department, through the Bureau of Population, Refugees, and Migration (PRM) and its Emergency Refugee and Migration Account; and the

- U.S. Department of Defense, through funds appropriated to the Office of Humanitarian and Refugee Affairs and disbursed by regional commands.

The president may also draw down Defense Department material and personnel assets to respond to disasters and instruct other agencies to contribute to the response.

reminders of Africa's recurrent and exceptional vulnerability to national disasters, just as violent eruptions in Congo-Brazzaville, Central African Republic, Guinea-Bissau, and Lesotho and the bloody war between Eritrea and Ethiopia demonstrate the depth of harm to Africa's civilian populations by man-made catastrophes. To these must now be added the mounting, profound strains of the HIV/AIDS pandemic on weak states and vulnerable societies.

The new administration will be called upon to respond to these humanitarian crises rapidly and visibly. Rendering aid to victims of disaster ranks high among U.S. national values and goals, and humanitarian assistance consistently attracts bipartisan support within Congress and reliable popular support from the American people. Conspicuous failure to respond effectively could damage the administration's standing, domestically and internationally, and invite accusations of callousness, ineptitude, and irresponsibility.

The Clinton administration responded quickly to the drought in the Horn and to floods in Mozambique. It demonstrated global leadership in mobilizing humanitarian resources to consolidate the Mozambique and Angolan peace accords, began to address the growing needs of HIV/AIDS orphans, and assisted victims of the Eritrea-Ethiopia border war. Nonetheless, there is growing recognition within the government and senior foreign policy circles that U.S. emergency assistance needs to be systematically strengthened, if it is to be more effective. Toward this end, the Bush administration should

- Articulate to Congress and the nation the moral case and national interests that call for a pragmatic, effective, and sustained U.S. humanitarian engagement in Africa.

- Strengthen the leadership and coherence of U.S. humanitarian programs to avoid redundancy and increase accountability.

- Heighten programmatic attention to human rights, protection of civilian populations, internally displaced persons, and the rule of law.

- Take concrete steps to mitigate unintended negative consequences of relief, including the gross diversion of humanitarian

Table 7.1
Total U.S. Government Humanitarian Assistance, 1988–1999
(millions of dollars)

	U.S. Government Humanitarian Aid			
Year	To Africa	To Africa as % of total	To rest of world	Total worldwide
1988	271.7	84	50.3	322.0
1989	182.4	56	145.9	328.3
1990	328.9	64	185.6	514.5
1991	527.7	43	701.6	514.5
1992	1,003.7	83	210.8	1,214.5
1993	656.1	61	419.9	1,076.0
1994	829.4	62	499.4	1,328.8
1995	569.7	68	264.5	834.2
1996	453.6	51	429.7	883.3
1997	508.2	58	369.5	877.7
1998	540.9	61	344.5	885.4
1999	681.3	45	824.5	1,505.8

Source: U.S. Agency for International Development (USAID), Office of U.S. Foreign Disaster Assistance (OFDA), *Annual Reports, FY1989–FY1999* (Washington, D.C.: USAID, 1989–1999).

Note: There is no single accounting of U.S. government emergency monies. The annual reports of USAID's Office of U.S. Foreign Disaster Assistance capture the emergency expenditures of USAID (OFDA, OTI, FFP, and the Africa Bureau), USDA, DOD (including as close an estimate as possible of DOD draw-down funds), and State/PRM.

assets by armed elements, the related political and logistical support that this assistance can provide authoritarian leaderships, and the further undermining of elements within society that are already marginalized by authoritarian leadership.

■ Clarify U.S. strategies in Africa's humanitarian flash zones—eastern Congo and southern Sudan; emergent crises in Zimbabwe, Kenya, Côte d'Ivoire, and Guinea—and devise new programmatic responses to the increasing mass humanitarian deprivations caused by HIV/AIDS.

RISING STAKES, RISING RISKS

Humanitarian assistance has become a predominant, lead dimension of U.S. foreign policy in responding to crises abroad. In dollar terms and in the perceived importance of humanitarian aid, the 1988 election of George Bush and the end of the Cold War was a turning point. U.S. government humanitarian expenditures in Africa quadrupled at the end of the Cold War, reaching an all-time high of just more than $1 billion in 1992. This total accounted for 83 percent of all humanitarian aid expended that year (see table 7.1). In the Clinton years, emergency aid to Africa oscillated between a low of $508 million in 1997 and a high of $829 million in 1994, the latter largely in response to the genocide in Rwanda. In relative terms, during the Clinton years Africa "weighed" heaviest in 1995 with 68 percent of total humanitarian aid and lightest in 1999 with 45 percent of the total.[1]

What accounted for the turnaround? In the 1990s, humanitarian aid was perceived as a quick alternative to cope with the communal violence, breakdown of state structures, and massive civilian displacement that proliferated after the Cold War ended. There was bipartisan support in Congress for ample humanitarian relief. Existing bureaucratic instruments at the State Department and USAID provided flexible, quick response mechanisms to bolster U.S. humanitarian leadership. The first Bush administration implemented and supported groundbreaking initiatives, such as Operation Lifeline Sudan (1989 to present), the intervention to establish safe havens in northern Iraq (1991), and the intervention in Somalia (1992–1994).

To varying degrees, these initiatives asserted the primacy of humanitarian interests over long-standing notions of sovereignty and territorial integrity.

The October 1993 deaths of 18 American soldiers in Mogadishu triggered a retreat by the Clinton administration from combining military and diplomatic approaches with humanitarian activism in Africa—a backing away from humanitarian intervention. The decisions to stand back as genocide swept across Rwanda and to adopt a cautious approach to successive crises that erupted in Liberia (1993, 1994, and 1996), eastern Zaire/Congo (1996, 1998 to the present), and Angola (1998 to the present) were heavily colored by U.S. experience in Somalia. Although humanitarian assistance continued in large amounts during all these crises, there was little linkage among military intervention, humanitarian initiatives, and political objectives. Humanitarian action became increasingly a means and an end unto itself, detached from the broader foreign policy context.

The administration would in 1999 move decidedly in the opposite direction in its humanitarian intervention in Kosovo, inviting allegations of a double standard and systematic neglect when the humanitarian crisis occurred in Africa. The March 2000 decision to dispatch 900 American soldiers to Mozambique (via South Africa) to assist victims of a sudden hurricane was in part a response to this criticism.

THE MIXED U.S. HUMANITARIAN RECORD IN AFRICA

During the Clinton years, U.S. leadership and substantial humanitarian relief saved many lives and alleviated much misery in Africa, continuing the tradition of previous administrations.

Within Congress and among the American public, strong bipartisan support for humanitarian assistance to Africa persists. Accordingly, U.S. financial commitments in the 1990s were impressive. With the exception of the Kosovo crisis of 1999, Africa has accounted for more than half of U.S. humanitarian expenditures worldwide. Technically, U.S. assistance has long been seen as responsive and professional. USAID's Office of Foreign Disaster Assistance is recognized as having an exceptional ability to respond swiftly and proactively with its field teams and to disburse monies far faster than other major donors. The State Department's Bureau of Population, Refugees, and Migration (PRM) is integral to United Nations operations, the International Committee of the Red Cross, and other multilateral and international humanitarian activities. Both USAID and the State Department have developed close working relationships with major U.S. NGOs.

But a closer look at several crises where the United States made substantial humanitarian investments reveals just how mixed the long-term impact has been. Although humanitarian aid certainly helped thousands survive in the short term, it does not address the root causes of conflict and poverty—that role is the responsibility of other parts of the foreign policy structures of the United States government. Relief assistance may be technically successful and redress an immediate moral imperative, but relief assistance by itself is politically insufficient. Indeed, humanitarian assistance dispersed under weak controls and accountability, and without regard to political ramifications or broader foreign policy goals, can run counter to U.S. interests. Recent examples abound of heavy U.S. humanitarian investments in Africa that led to disappointment:

Somalia. Some observers contend that the U.S. intervention in 1992 to 1993 saved over 300,000 lives (although this claim remains the subject of considerable debate). But the October 1993 debacle damaged the image of humanitarian intervention, all but scuttling the subsequent use of the U.S. military to support humanitarian operations in Africa.

Rwanda. The United States failed to prevent, end, or mitigate the 1994 genocide, despite repeated warnings and requests for assistance from local and international human rights groups, UN peacekeeping forces, and international relief organizations.

Eastern Zaire/Congo. International humanitarian support to refugee camps controlled by those responsible for the 1994 Rwanda genocide amounted to more than $2 billion between 1994 and early 1997, of which the U.S. share was approximately $500 million. Over time, this humanitarian expenditure strengthened the armed factions that dominated the refugee camps—those who were in fact responsible for the genocide—and thereby stoked violent instability in the

Great Lakes region, contributing to the deaths of tens of thousands of civilians. Since 1996, the United States has been unable and unwilling to curb war crimes and human rights abuses by the Rwandan and Ugandan militaries and their proxy forces in eastern Congo.

Angola. From 1992 to 1998, the United States bilaterally and multi-laterally invested more than $100 million per year (and in some years more than $200 million) to ease mass suffering (particularly during the intense fighting from 1992 to 1994 and subsequently to facilitate the return home of 3 million internally displaced persons). The collapse of the Lusaka peace process in 1998 led to the immediate displacement of 1 million Angolans and a sharp deterioration of humanitarian access to war-affected communities.

Sudan. Since 1989, the United States has invested more than $1.5 billion in humanitarian relief into Sudan, concentrated in the south. This investment has had no effective linkage to a peace process; the administration, along with other donors, was unable to mitigate and prepare for the 1998 famine; and U.S. plans to provide aid directly to the rebel Sudanese People's Liberation Army (SPLA) have met with substantial opposition on the part of some NGOs and have invited escalating demands from the armed insurgents for direct control over the management of humanitarian assets. In May 2001 President Bush named USAID administrator Andrew Natsios the humanitarian co-ordinator for Sudan, and Natsios immediately formed a Sudan Task Force within USAID to review and better coordinate U.S. policy. During Secretary Powell's May trip to Africa, Natsios announced that the United States would commit an additional $60 million in humanitarian relief, including a significant share to drought victims in the north. These moves occurred during a review of U.S. policy toward Sudan that came down in favor of a cautious, incremental effort to promote a negotiated just settlement to Sudan's 18-year internal war. That approach requires critical engagement with Khartoum and an even-handed approach to the government and opposition. It awaits, however, the appointment of a special envoy.

Liberia. During the civil war, massive U.S. humanitarian assistance was critical to the survival of many war-affected Liberians but did not compensate for U.S. unwillingness to engage on the political and military front. From 1996 to 1997, U.S. humanitarian and transitional assistance supported a peace process that culminated in the election of Charles Taylor as president. Although that brought short-term peace to Liberia, over time Taylor has extended his destabilizing actions beyond Liberia to Sierra Leone and Guinea.

Sierra Leone. Over the past eight years, $300 million in U.S. government humanitarian aid has not stemmed a steady deterioration of the humanitarian situation; the United States is perceived as having pressed an inherently flawed Lomé peace agreement upon the signatories in July 1999. When the Revolutionary United Front resumed hostilities in May 2000, that accord subsequently collapsed, ushering in a renewed humanitarian emergency.

Burundi. An estimated $200 million of U.S. humanitarian assistance (from 1993 through the summer of 2000) has contained but not stifled violence and widespread suffering. In the meantime the Arusha process languishes.

These recent experiences do not argue that the United States can, or should, turn away from humanitarian engagement in Africa. Nor is it realistic to expect that the Bush administration will resort to military humanitarian intervention in Africa. Rather, there are realistic, achievable and meaningful steps that the Bush administration can take to strengthen the effectiveness of its humanitarian programs. The Bush administration is best advised to pay attention to four priorities:

■ *Outline to Congress and the nation the continued moral case and national interests behind a pragmatic, focused humanitarian engagement in Africa, despite the many failings and obstacles to success.*

■ *Strengthen the institutional coherence and leadership of U.S. humanitarian assistance to overcome redundancy, fragmentation, and lack of accountability, without doing harm to existing emergency delivery-mechanisms.*

■ *Address programmatically within U.S. humanitarian policy how to strengthen human rights, end the culture of impunity, and ensure*

protection of internally displaced persons and other vulnerable ci-
vilians.

- *Devise coherent and feasible strategies for humanitarian flash zones—southern Sudan, Angola, eastern Congo, and emergent challenges in Kenya, Côte d'Ivoire, and Zimbabwe—while introducing new programs to ameliorate the mass humanitarian suffering caused by the HIV/AIDS pandemic.*

ARTICULATING THE CASE FOR HUMANITARIAN ENGAGEMENT IN AFRICA

The Bush administration will be called upon to respond effectively to humanitarian crises in Africa, even while it resists any military commitments to these crisis areas. Current and future crises, popular and congressional constituencies for humanitarian assistance, and media interest will sustain pressure. To shape expectations, the Bush administration should articulate two critical dimensions of U.S. humanitarian action in Africa:

Moral leadership. The United States is a nation of strong values of generosity and of problem solving. A basic tenet of our society is its commitment to alleviate suffering in the world. Upholding basic American values—the primacy of the rule of law and the unacceptability of violence, the right to be free of repression, the right to the pursuit of economic and spiritual fulfillment—and seeing these values gain ground are a vital national interest. Nowhere are these values more tested than in Africa.

U.S. national interests. Beyond immediate moral responsibility, the United States has a high stake in increased global stability. This stake has components that are political, military, and economic, and relates to such transnational considerations as trade, security and terrorism, drugs, and immigration. It also includes the impact of instability on U.S. allies around the world. Nowhere is there greater instability than in Africa.

Clearly articulating these arguments will demonstrate that, despite the inherent obstacles to stemming Africa's crises quickly and the high risk of setbacks and failure, on moral and national interest grounds the United States has little choice but to persevere, make its response more pragmatic, focused, and effective, and seek simultaneously to address both the causes and symptoms of humanitarian crises.

LEADERSHIP AND INSTITUTIONAL COHERENCE OF U.S. HUMANITARIAN AID

As humanitarian relief has grown more central to the U.S. government's response to a number of crises, attention has shifted increasingly to the question of how to strengthen the leadership and coherence of humanitarian policies without harming existing capacities.

Several recurrent criticisms have been voiced in recent years. Because there is no empowered senior humanitarian voice, humanitarian concerns are typically not integrated into policy debate at senior levels, with the result that the humanitarian implications of political and military decisions are not adequately weighed. Fragmented institutional responsibilities for U.S. humanitarian programs lead to politically costly delays and generate insufficient leverage with allies. Coordination among the various entities that administer U.S. humanitarian aid—the Department of State, USAID, and the Pentagon—is often ad hoc. The formally designated institutional coordinator for foreign disasters—the USAID administrator—usually cannot devote the time required because of the day-to-day responsibilities involved in managing USAID; moreover, as the head of a second-tier agency, that individual lacks the authority to coordinate other agencies. Thus, although, humanitarian assistance is a major facet of U.S. foreign policy, effectively no one is in charge. This lack of institutional coherence and leadership undercuts the ability of the administration to articulate effectively to an international audience, in a clear and timely fashion, what is at stake and what form of international response is required.

No easy or guaranteed institutional solutions will bring immediate, heightened coherence and leadership to humanitarian programs. One of the more fiercely debated initiatives, in what would be a complex institutional undertaking, is the formal amalgamation of the government's civilian humanitarian programs, either under the aegis of the State Department or USAID, or as a separate federal agency. In the absence of agreement over amalgamation, discrete steps can be taken to enhance coordination across different agencies, though these measures will have limited benefits. More robust measures can be pursued to identify more clearly who will lead on humanitarian policy and empower that individual accordingly.

Regardless of what measures the incoming administration pursues, positive returns can only come through sustained effort, at a high level, that systematically experiments to determine what best mix of policies and institutional innovations can improve U.S. humanitarian performance.

FORGING A BROADER U.S. HUMANITARIAN AGENDA

The Bush administration will face a conundrum: Humanitarian needs in Africa will increase, while ongoing crises persist. Resources and mechanisms, including willing and able NGO implementers, will make heavy reliance on humanitarian action a relatively easy choice.

But this trend will invite controversy. The realization that excessive reliance on emergency aid offers imperfect, unsustainable, and sometimes destabilizing solutions is growing. Rwanda and the experience of the Kivu camps showed that there are crises where humanitarian relief can be destabilizing. These analyses are spreading in humanitarian circles. Similar currents of thought are also growing among observers of the humanitarian relief community: in "industry" watchdogs, in academia, and in the press. As a result, U.S. humanitarian policies in Africa are increasingly being called to task. Finally, misgivings about humanitarian aid are taking hold in the government itself. At the operational level, there has been a growing interest in "do-no-harm" approaches and a growing determination to provide more appropriate aid.

To address these concerns requires broadening current approaches to humanitarian action on three fronts: incorporating a stronger human rights and protection component in humanitarian operations; addressing the issue of internally displaced persons; and building the capacity to think through the political repercussions of humanitarian strategies.

Bring human rights into the humanitarian agenda

The realization that the mere provision of relief is an insufficient response to many complex crises is on the increase. Proliferating emergencies make Africa the dominant battleground for progress in the fight against war crimes, the establishment of justice as a political deterrent against instability, and generally for projecting the message that accountability is an integral part of foreign policy.

Nowhere has that realization dawned more starkly than in the successive crises in the Great Lakes. Beyond the appalling human toll, the 1994 genocide in Rwanda was highly detrimental to U.S. interests: it destabilized the entire region for years to come, fueling and even igniting violence at the local and regional level. For the United States, its aftermath has been and continues to be costly to manage, both financially and diplomatically. It forced the United States into an unquestioning, yet unrewarding, alliance with the unrepresentative government of a tiny country, Rwanda—an alliance that hamstrung the Clinton administration's broader diplomatic efforts in the region. Finally, the United States faced considerable political and diplomatic criticism for its failure to play a more active role in mitigating the murderous events of 1994. Today few people challenge the view that an earlier and more activist political response to the genocide would have better served the interests of the United States, the victims, and the stability and prosperity of the region.

The current crisis in eastern Congo, rooted in the events of 1994, is a further case in point. According to David Scheffer, the State Department's former ambassador-at-large for war crimes, "The worst humanitarian crisis in the world is a silent one." It is a crisis for which relief aid does not provide a solution. First, access is a nigh insurmountable problem—the security and physical environment is so difficult that aid agencies simply cannot reach the affected populations. Second, it is becoming increasingly clear that the relief these agencies might provide would have little impact on the suffering and certainly not make a dent in the cause of the suffering—the murderous to and fro of marauding military and paramilitary formations.

A promising new tack in U.S. policy was seen in the late 2000 visit of a joint State Department–National Security Council team to the

Great Lakes. The team emphasized a commitment not simply to address the consequences of violence, but to address some of its root causes and stem the culture of impunity that potentially fuels its recurrence. In this instance, the United States took its Rwandan and Ugandan allies to task over the conduct of their militaries and their role in exacerbating conflict and demonstrated U.S. support to the International Criminal Tribunal for Rwanda (ICTR), the grassroots conflict-resolution Gacaca mechanisms in Rwanda, and the Rwanda Survivors Fund. These initiatives have resulted in a humanitarian agenda that attempts to build accountability through programs to empower civil society and through military justice programs. They send a clear message that the United States will not tolerate impunity and will in certain cases support an international judicial effort, should the various actors prove unwilling to take action themselves.

Better manage the negative consequences of humanitarian action

For years, questions have arisen concerning the role and unintended consequences of relief aid in the midst of violent conflict. Does humanitarian aid exacerbate or prolong conflicts? What are the political repercussions of relief programs on the ground? What are the limits of humanitarian neutrality?

These are particularly difficult questions for U.S. policymakers, and the Bush administration will have to deal with them. However, no single office, department, or bureau in government is tasked with gauging the political repercussions of humanitarian programs. Such analyses may be factored in from time to time, with varying degrees of success, but experience shows that senior foreign policy officials are seldom successful at it.

Failure to conduct this kind of analysis can be costly. First, U.S. humanitarian efforts may prove in some cases detrimental to stated U.S. policy aims. Second, if the government does not analyze the political repercussions of its aid, others will, and their analysis will be public. The administration risks vocal criticism of its humanitarian assistance from academia, NGO partners, think tanks and watchdog groups, the press, and Congress.

Devise a workable, coherent policy toward internally displaced persons

Another part of the challenge of forging a broader humanitarian agenda, and one of the more thorny issues likely to confront the new administration, is how to help people who have been displaced by conflict, but remain within the borders of their country of origin and thus do not meet the legal definition of refugees. Of the estimated 35 million people affected by internal conflict worldwide, 20 million are internally displaced persons (IDPs). No international organization or UN agency has a clear mandate to assist the internally displaced, with either relief or protection. And what assistance IDPs do receive is made more difficult by the fact that local authorities in control are often uncooperative, the environment unsettled and access problematic. Political problems of sovereignty are also overwhelming. Yet, although inherently hard to pin down with any degree of certainty, the number of IDPs in Africa is staggering: an estimated 4.5 million in Sudan, one-half of whom are in Khartoum; 1.5 to 1.8 million in Congo; up to 700,000 in Eritrea; an estimated 1.5 million in Sierra Leone (one-third of the country's population); 3 million in Angola; and 750,000 in Burundi.

The problem of international responsibility for IDPs remains unsolved. A high-ranking UN commission has been tasked to investigate further. But given the inherent problems with intervening on behalf of people who remain under the jurisdiction of their own government, it is clear that addressing the IDP issue will require a commitment both to protecting displaced persons and to tackling the root causes of displacement.

HUMANITARIAN FLASH ZONES

The Bush administration needs coherent, feasible humanitarian approaches for several priority crises.

Sudan. The war with southern rebels has gone on since 1983. It is estimated that in this period 2 million have died and 4 million have been displaced. A major challenge for the Bush administration will include rethinking Operation Lifeline Sudan—which, despite some successes, has been ineffective and at times even counterproductive by seeming to encourage intransigence on the part of all the warring parties—and reassessing direct transitional support (the STAR program) to opposition groups; the support, while minimal, has fed the perception in Khartoum that the United States is waging a covert war on behalf of the rebels. Administration programs that rely on and strengthen local capacity should be clearly linked to U.S policy goals. Overall, U.S. humanitarian assistance to southern Sudan, annually exceeding $100 million, will need careful management to avoid large-scale diversions to war aims.

Democratic Republic of Congo. Early in 2000, a study sponsored by the International Rescue Committee claimed that, since the beginning of the last war in eastern Congo, up to 1.7 million had lost their lives as a direct or indirect result of the fighting, and 1.8 million are IDPs. Abuses by all sides against civilian populations have been massive and widespread. Should Rwanda and Uganda, ostensible U.S. "partners," be revealed as complicit in these atrocities, the Bush administration will find it very difficult to stand by idly. However, laudable efforts are currently under way to explore appropriate forms of relief—programs that will not exacerbate the conflict—and link them to broader humanitarian goals: civil society empowerment, protection, justice, and accountability. The Bush administration should continue, and expand, support for these efforts.

Angola. Up to 1 million people have been displaced since fighting between the government and UNITA broke out afresh in 1998. Although government forces have been fairly successful in the past two years in marginalizing UNITA, an outright military victory does not appear near, and UNITA forces have been reverting to guerrilla tactics in areas under government control, causing further turmoil for the civilian population. Many of those affected do not receive relief assistance because of access problems and because, as IDPs, no organization has a clear mandate for them. The Bush administration should increase efforts to use the very strong and activist Angolan church networks to deliver assistance, empowering them in their bid to force peace and dialogue on the warring parties.

Burundi and Sierra Leone. Both countries are in complete upheaval, with tremendous humanitarian dislocation and suffering. Conflict has resulted in approximately 600,000 refugees and 750,000 internally displaced in Burundi and 500,000 refugees and between 500,000 and 1 million internally displaced in Sierra Leone. In both countries, the Clinton administration encouraged the warring parties to reach peace agreements, with disastrous results. In both cases, it is clear that a lasting political settlement, not relief assistance, is what will bring real relief to the people.

LOOMING EXPLOSIONS

Worsening crises are possible in Zimbabwe, Kenya, Côte d'Ivoire, and Guinea. All, except Guinea, were considered the hopeful countries among the newly independent African nations, and undergirded political and economic stability at the subregional level. And all, including Guinea, share a further common trait—dismally corrupt and unaccountable governance—that has slowly run them into the ground. That is why it is essential that, should it become necessary (and it already is in Guinea and Kenya), U.S. humanitarian assistance go further than just relief—that it actively help empower forces for change in these countries, that it be linked to broader political goals, and that it do nothing to strengthen the regimes in place.

Even more unavoidable will be the cumulative impact of the already unfolding HIV/AIDS pandemic. Of the world's 25 most HIV/AIDS-affected countries, 24 are in Africa, and during the Bush administration, the epidemic will reshape every level of African societies with devastating effect. Although this is far too grave an issue to be treated with a predominantly humanitarian response, it cannot be neglected. There are already an estimated 13 million AIDS orphans in Africa; this number is expected to surge to 42 million in the next nine years. The impact on social services and the economy will gravely strain, if not overwhelm, government capacities. The food security of households will undergo dramatic changes. These problems may contribute to a worsening of existing political crises, as in Zimbabwe, or threaten the achievements of more stable countries, such as

Botswana. U.S. humanitarian assistance will be a necessary part of a much larger effort to mitigate the social and economic effects of the pandemic, including the potential for escalating violence, in a manner consistent with broader HIV/AIDS interventions.

RECOMMENDATIONS

- *Build increased institutional coherence and leadership in U.S. humanitarian policy, without constraining flexible humanitarian responses.*

The Bush administration should move to enact swift institutional and procedural reforms while being careful to avoid stifling creativity or quick action through excessive red tape or top-heavy bureaucratic structures.

- *Broaden the definition of humanitarian assistance. The Bush administration should broaden the concept of humanitarian assistance to encompass civilian protection, human rights, and mechanisms of accountability, including military justice programs and international and national tribunals.*

Other donors look to the United States to provide leadership on these issues. Practically, the United States should continue support to the International Criminal Tribunal for Rwanda; support the creation of a treaty-based special court in Sierra Leone and potentially in Burundi; support the creation of an African regional criminal court; commit $30 million to $40 million to the State Department's Office of War Crimes Issues; provide financial aid to victim reparation schemes such as the Truth and Reconciliation Commission programs in South Africa; and, as the Clinton administration did in Rwanda, not hesitate to use U.S. leverage in multilateral organizations to back up the message that accountability is a central feature of the administration's foreign policy.

- *Tie humanitarian programs to foreign policy objectives; take practical steps to measure the political repercussions of relief programs; and implement do-no-harm strategies.*

The size of humanitarian operations does not equate to effectiveness in assisting disaster victims and promoting U.S. interests. Humanitarian response alone cannot address the causes of a crisis. The Bush administration should strive to design humanitarian assistance programs that are appropriate to needs and promote positive developments in the crisis at hand, or, at the very least, do no harm. The Bush administration should decide on practical steps to measure the overall contribution of U.S. humanitarian assistance, with a special emphasis on minimizing diversion of humanitarian aid into the hands of armed elements.

■ *Provide leadership to ensure the creation of mechanisms for protection and assistance to the internally displaced.*

The Bush administration should build on recent efforts by the representative of the UN secretary general on internally displaced persons to change norms and mandates of international organizations to enhance protection of, and access to, IDPs. The administration should take the lead in creating legislative and operational frameworks within the U.S. government to more systematically address the IDP issue.

■ *Clarify U.S. humanitarian policy toward the most challenging, politically charged, and controversial humanitarian crises in Sudan, eastern Congo, and Angola.*

The Bush administration should give particular attention to these three cases, where the magnitude of the crises is staggering, where it will face inherited controversy over U.S. humanitarian policy and its political consequences, and where there will be continued public and media scrutiny of U.S. efforts.

■ *Brace for crises in Kenya, Zimbabwe, Cote d'Ivoire, and Guinea.*

The new administration should address these potential crises with an integrated policy that combines diplomatic action, support to forces of change, and humanitarian assistance. Relying on humanitarian assistance alone will not prevent or mitigate a deteriorating situation in any of these countries, nor will it help improve things if the situation spirals out of control.

■ *Respond to the new humanitarian demands borne of HIV/AIDS.*

In the next four years the HIV/AIDS pandemic will generate millions of orphans and radically interfere with food production throughout

Africa. The Bush administration should mobilize its senior humanitarian officials to analyze the malnutrition consequences of HIV/AIDS and devise robust new humanitarian programs to mitigate them.

Note

[1] It should be noted, however, that large amounts of money were spent during the Clinton years in the form of contributions to regional peacekeeping and Department of Defense expenditures. U.S. contributions to UN specialized agencies involved in crisis response are included.

INDEX

Abacha, Sani, 75, 76, 80, 81
Abiola, Masood, 81
Abubakar, Abdulsalami, 76, 81
Afewerki, Isaias, 41
African Center for Strategic Studies (ACSS), 52, 58–59
African Crisis Response Force (ACRF), 57–58, 91
African Crisis Response Initiative (ACRI), 1, 2, 52, 58, 91
African Growth and Opportunity Act (AGOA), 1, 2, 9, 98–99, 101, 112–114
Aid to Africa: development assistance, 117–118; needed resources for African countries, 116–117; recommendations for U.S., 118–119; in U.S. policy, 115–116. *See also* Debt relief; Development assistance; Humanitarian assistance; U.S. Agency for International Development (USAID)
Albright, Madeleine, 81
Algerian oil exports, 107–108

Algiers accord. See Eritrea-Ethiopia
Angola: conflict and failed peace process in, 38, 43, 62; HIV infection rates in, 18; human rights abuses in, 48; intervention in the Congo, 36; oil production in future, 107; priority crisis in, 35, 135; as source of U.S. oil imports, 6; UN efforts in, 44; U.S. investment in, 127
Annan, Kofi, 14, 23, 45, 77
Anti-Corruption Commission, Nigeria, 83
Arusha peace process, 37–38, 42
Bedie, Henri Konan, 39
Binational Commission (BNC), U.S.–South African, 83, 90, 93
Botswana: Merck-Gates Foundation HIV/AIDS-related agreement with, 21; prevalence of HIV infections in, 18
Bouteflika, Abdelaziz, 36, 77
Brown, Ron, 88
Burundi: Arusha peace process,

37–38, 42; interethnic violence in, 43, 62; priority crisis in, 35, 136; U.S. humanitarian assistance to, 128

Bush, George W., 14

Bush administration: advice on leadership role in Africa, 8; Africa-related priorities for, 59–63, 122, 128–129; engagement in Africa, 2, 4; focus of policy tasks of, xi; HIV/AIDS-related recommendations for, 27–31; inherited African problems, 43; need for humanitarian approaches for priority crises, 134–136; needs security policies, 56; need to address USAID status, 117; outlines for policy in Sudan, 34–35; policy challenges in Kenya, 39–40; recommendations for bilateral policy in South Africa, 93–95; recommendations to strengthen U.S. emergency assistance, 122, 124; recommended funding for Africa by, 99, 101–102; recommended goals related to HIV/AIDS, 15–22; recommended leadership role in Africa, 53–54; recommended policy for African humanitarian assistance, 122–123, 129–134; South African challenges to, 86. *See also* Foreign policy, U.S.

Bush (G.H.W.) administration, 124–125

Cameroon: Chad-Cameroon oil pipeline, 6, 108; oil resources in, 108; political instability in, 62–63

Centers for Disease Control and Prevention (CDC), 20

Central African region: conflict in, 46; as source of U.S. oil imports, 6

Central African Republic, 43

Chad: Chad-Cameroon oil pipeline, 6, 108; crisis in, 43; oil reserves of, 107–108; political instability in, 62–63

Clinton, Bill: address to National Summit on Africa, 19; meeting with de Klerk and Mandela in United States, 88; trip to Africa (1998), 19, 40, 91; visit to Nigeria (2000), 19, 40, 82

Clinton administration: achievements in Africa, 40–43, 86–93, 97–99, 114; African crisis agenda during, 43; Africa-related programs and regional offices, 114; attention to conflict resolution in Africa, 40–43; Binational Commission established by, 9; collaboration with European allies on Africa, 42–43; emergency and humanitarian aid to Africa during, 124–125; engagement in Africa by, 1–2; Kenyan policy of, 40; military outreach to African countries, 58; policies toward Nigeria and South Africa, 74; policy initiatives in, 4; policy toward Sudan, 37, 48; position on African debt relief, 108; provision of military

Clinton administration (*continued*)
training in Africa, 70; reactive
policy for Africa, 57; relationship with Mbeki, 92–93; response to humanitarian crises
in Africa, 122; role in South
Africa, 86–93; support for
African debt relief initiatives,
98, 105; White House AIDS
Policy Office, 20, 28. *See also*
Foreign policy, U.S.
Conflicts in Africa: Clinton administration conflict resolution, 40–43; Nigerian role in
resolution of, 77; potential in
Côte d'Ivoire, 62; potential in
Kenya, 62; potential in Zimbabwe, 62; regional, 46; in 1990s,
33; Uganda and Senegal, 40;
U.S. foreign policy as root
cause of, 127; U.S. leadership
role, 67–68
Congo-Brazzaville, 46, 62, 107
Congress: Bush administration
dialogue about Africa with, 54;
humanitarian assistance drawn
from appropriations of, 121;
introduction of and debate
about AGOA, 112–113; support
for humanitarian assistance, 122
Corporate Council on Africa, 1
Côte d'Ivoire: coup d'état (1999),
39; crisis in, 43, 136; potential
for conflict in, 62
Crisis prevention: U.S. role in, 49–
52
Debt: debtor countries in Africa,
96; external debt of African
countries, 96, 102–103; owed

to United States by African
countries, 105; U.S. forgiveness
of some African, 105
Debt relief: HIPC framework for,
103–104; reason for, 4; recommendations about, 106; required, 97, 99; U.S. policy
toward African, 103
de Klerk, F.W., 88
Democratic Republic of Congo:
civil war in, 36, 46–47; crisis in
eastern, 132; Lusaka process in,
36–37, 45–46, 57; oil resources
in, 107; political instability in,
62–63; priority crisis in, 60–61,
135; requirement for U.S. engagement in, 34; UN operation
in, 57; U.S. support for refugee
camps in, 126–127
Development assistance: to Africa,
112; recommendations for
U.S., 118–119; from United
States to Africa, 115–118
Displaced persons in Africa, 134
DRC. See Democratic Republic of
Congo
East African Community, 69
ECOMOG: effectiveness in regional operations, 69; management of Abuja process, 42;
needs encouragement, 59;
Nigerian peacekeeping efforts
under, 79, 84; U.S. peacekeeping through, 80
Equatorial Guinea: oil reserves of,
107–108; as source of U.S. oil
imports, 6
Eritrea: alliance of United States
with, 2; war with Ethiopia, 36

Eritrea-Ethiopia: border war, 2, 44, 61–62; peace agreement (2001), 34, 36; requires U.S. leadership, 44; UN peacekeeping in, 44–45, 61; U.S. support for peace operation in, 57

Ethiopia: alliance of United States with, 2; HIV infection rates in, 18; political instability in, 62–63; war between Eritrea and, 36. *See also* Eritrea-Ethiopia

Evertz, Scott, 23, 28

Export-Import Bank: efforts in Africa, 9–10; HIV/AIDS-related export purchase guarantee, 20

Foreign policy, U.S.: of Clinton administration in Africa, 41–42, 57–59, 86–93; for crisis prevention in Africa, 49–52; effect of HIV/AIDS pandemic on, 5–6, 13–14; HIV/AIDS will reshape, 13–14; humanitarian assistance to Africa, 120, 123–131; recommendation for security policy in Africa, 71–73; requires collaboration with allies and UN, 12; responsibility for root causes of African conflict and poverty, 126; for Sudan, 48; toward Africa, x; toward HIV/AIDS in Africa, 18–21; toward Nigeria, 80–82; worldwide humanitarian assistance (1988–1999), 120, 123, 125

Fowler Commission, 51

Gabon oil exports, 107–108

Gbagbo, Laurent, 39

Ghana: HIV infection rates in, 18

Gore, Al, 90

Great Lakes region: crises in, 132; U.S. State Department–NSC visit to, 132–133

Guei, Robert, 39

Guinea: crisis in, 43, 136; instability and violence in, 40, 62–63

Guinea-Bissau: crisis in, 43; political instability in, 62–63

Heavily Indebted Poor Countries (HIPC) Initiative, 10, 98, 101, 103–105

HIV/AIDS: global trust fund for, 14, 77; mobilization to combat, 1; in Nigeria, 75–77, 79, 84; recommendations to combat African, 27–31; requirements to reduce infection rates, 16; United Nations UNAIDS program on, 7–8, 20–22; U.S. humanitarian assistance to mitigate effects of, 137; U.S. LIFE initiative for global, 19

HIV/AIDS pandemic: Africa in context of global, 5–6, 13; impact of, 136; scope and nature in Africa, 17–18; U.S. policy toward global, 18–19

Holbrooke, Richard, 36, 40

Humanitarian assistance: leadership and institutional coherence of U.S., 130–131; political goals of U.S., 136; recommendations for United States Africa-related, 137–139; of United States to Africa and world, 120–121. *See also* HIV/AIDS; Specific countries

Humanitarian emergencies: effect of U.S. failure to respond to, viii

IFIs. See International financial institutions (IFIs)

Inter-Congolese Dialogue, 47

Intergovernmental Authority on Development (IGAD): lack of collective military capability, 69; peace process in Sudan, 45–46; peace process of, 37

International financial institutions (IFIs): attention to HIPC relief process, 104. *See also* International Monetary Fund (IMF); World Bank

International Monetary Fund (IMF): proposes HIPC (1996), 103; standby agreement with Nigeria, 82

Investment: African-related U.S. policy, 111–114; recommendations related to African, 114–115; U.S. foreign direct investment, 75

Jackson, Jesse, 35

Johnston, Harry, 37

Joint Economic Policy Council (JEPC), U.S.-Nigerian, 82, 83

Kabila, Joseph, 47

Kabila, Laurent, 36, 42, 46

Kagame, Paul, 41

Kenya: bombing of U.S. embassy in, 7; Clinton administration policy toward, 40; crisis in, 43, 136; potential for conflict in, 62; problems in, 39–40

Lake, Anthony, 36, 40

Leadership and Investment in

Fighting an Epidemic (LIFE), 19

Lesotho: crisis in, 43; political instability in, 62–63

Liberia: political instability in, 62–63; proposed war crimes tribunal for, 44; Taylor administration in, 35, 51, 79; threat of renewed war in, 40; UN embargo on, 35–36, 44; U.S. humanitarian assistance to, 127–128

Lomé peace agreement: Clinton response to collapse of, 2; U.S. role urging acceptance of, 35

Lusaka peace process, 35–38, 45–46

McHenry, Donald, 81

Mandela, Nelson, 25, 38, 40, 87, 88, 91

Masire, Ketumile, 36

Mbeki, Thabo, 24, 45, 77, 85, 90, 92–93

Millennium Africa Renaissance Program (MAP), 77, 97

Moi, Daniel arap, 40

Mozambique: peace process in, 40; U.S. contribution to transition in, 1

Mugabe, Robert, xi, 39

Multinational companies: investment in African oil resources, 107; problems in Africa of U.S., 108–109

Museveni, Yoweri, 41

Namibia: HIV infection rates in, 18; intervention in the Congo, 36

National Summit on Africa, 1

National Union for the Total Independence of Angola (UNITA), 38, 51

Natsios, Andrew, 127
Niger Delta Development Commission, 77
Nigeria: Anti-Corruption Commission, 83; as candidate for partnership with United States, 73–74; Clinton administration policy toward, 74; corruption and weak institutions in, 75–76; democratization process in, 40, 43, 73–77; economic performance under Obasanjo administration, 76–77; HIV infection rate in, 18; military sector in, 78; need for U.S. bilateral relations with, 73–85; oil production in future, 107; oil reserves of, 74; People's Democratic Party (PDP), 79–80; political instability in, 62–63; recommended U.S. role in, 9; as regional hegemon, 74; role in conflict resolution in Africa, 77; as source of U.S. oil imports, 6; standby agreement with IMF, 82; strengthening U.S. bilateral relations with, 7; U.S. contribution to transition in, 1; U.S. engagement in, viii; U.S. foreign direct investment in, 75; weaknesses in, 78
Nongovernmental organizations (NGOs): critical of debt relief, 104; criticism of major oil companies, 109; debt cancellation argument, 104; weak administrative capacity of, 25
Nyerere, Julius, 37

Obasanjo, Olusegun, 14, 25, 45, 76–79, 82, 83
Oil industry, Africa: Algerian exports, 107–108; Angola, 6, 107; Chad-Cameroon, 6, 107–108; in Equatorial Guinea, 6, 107–108; future Angolan production, 107; Gabon's exports, 107–108; in Nigeria, 6, 74, 107; oil reserves, 107; oil resources of Sudan, 108; sources of U.S. supply, 6, 107; West African sources, 6
Operation Lifeline Sudan, 124
Organization of African Unity (OAU): "Committee of Ten," 39; Summit on HIV/AIDS, 25
Ouattara, Alassane, 39
Overseas Private Investment Corporation (OPIC), 9–10
Paris Club: arrangements for African debt reduction, 103; proposals for poor countries (1988–1996), 103
Partnership for Economic Growth and Opportunity in Africa, 113
Peace initiatives, Africa: Abuja process, 42; Arusha process, 42; IGAD initiative, 42, 45; Lomé agreement, 42; Lusaka process, 42, 45–47
Peacekeeping: absence in Rwanda of mission for, 2; Brahimi report on, ix; Nigerian contributions to, 79; strengthening of regional and UN, 68–69; through ECOMOG, 79–80, 84; by UN in Eritrea-Ethiopia, 44–45, 61; by UN in Sierra Leone,

resources in, 108; opportunities for positive impact in, 34; priority crisis in, 134–135; recommended U.S. policy in, 48; U.S. investment in, 127

Tambo, Oliver, 88

Tanzania, 7

Taylor, Charles, 35, 51, 79

Terrorism, international: in Africa's conflict-ridden areas, 56; shift in modality and structure of, 7

Trade, international: African Growth and Opportunity Act, 112–113; recommendations for U.S.-African, 114–115; requirement to refine rules on key drugs, 31; U.S. policy related to, 111–114. *See also* Oil industry, Africa

Uganda: alliance of United States with, 2; conflicts in, 40; intervention in the Congo, 36

UNITA. See National Union for the Total Independence of Angola (UNITA)

United Nations: AIDS conference in Lusaka (1999), 25; embargo on Liberia, 35–36; future of peacekeeping in Africa, 43; needs U.S. support for peacekeeping in Africa, 70–71; new peacekeeping operations in Africa, 59; Nigerian peacekeeping efforts within, 84; peacekeeping in Eritrea-Ethiopia, 34, 36; peacekeeping in Sierra Leone, 34, 44; Program on HIV/AIDS (UNAIDS), 7–8,

20–22; reform of its peacekeeping operations, 70–71; Sierra Leone on agenda of, 35–36. *See also* Peacekeeping

United States: acceptance of leadership role in Africa, 44; bilateral relations with South Africa and Nigeria, 73–95; citizens of Nigerian origin in, 75; contributions to UN peacekeeping in Africa, 59; developments shaping interests in Africa, 4–7; factors undermining African interests of, 55–56; funding of commitments to HIPC, 105; interests in Africa, 3–9, 96–99; leadership role in African conflicts, 67–68; moral responsibility in Africa, 129; need to collaborate with Nigerian on HIV/AIDS, 84; need to invest in Nigerian electoral process, 84–85; post–Cold War waning bilateral influence, 4–5; priority advisories for engagement in Africa, 10–12; program to enhance West African regional peacekeeping, 82; question of security operations role in Africa, 64–72; recommendation for building competent African national armies, 69–70; requirement to support UN peacekeeping operations, 70–71; reshaping of interests in, 4–7; sharing peacekeeping burden in Africa, 68; spending on HIV-infected people, 19. *See also* Bush administration;

United States *(continued)*
Clinton administration; Congress; Foreign policy, U.S.; U.S. Agency for International Development (USAID)
U.S. Agency for International Development (USAID): Africa Bureau, 117; closing of some missions in Africa, 50; closure of missions in Africa, 41; estimates of HIV prevention requirements, 22; funds allocated for Africa (1990s), 116; issue of institutional standing of, 117; need for new approach to Africa, 117; Office of Foreign Disaster Assistance, 125; Office of Transition Initiatives, 50, 52, 85
U.S. Department of Energy, 109
U.S. Department of State: Africa Bureau, 41, 50; Bureau of Population, Refugees, and Migration, 126

U.S. Department of Transportation, 113
U.S. Trade Representative (USTR): efforts in Africa, 9–10; U.S. policy on pharmaceuticals, 23
Viljoen, Constand, 89
West Africa: Jackson's trips to, 35; regionalized conflict in, 46; as source of U.S. oil imports, 6; U.S. contribution to peacekeeping efforts in, 82
Wolpe, Howard, 38, 42
World Bank: proposes HIPC (1996), 103; role in Chad-Cameroon pipeline development, 108; Trust Fund, 20
Zairian refugee camps, 126–27
Zenawi, Meles, 41
Zimbabwe: crisis in, 44, 136; increased internal tensions, 38–39; intervention in Congo, 36; Mugabe's behavior in, xi; potential for conflict in, 62; requires priority attention, 34, 44

ABOUT THE CONTRIBUTORS

NAN BORTON has worked for more than 30 years in foreign assistance programs, with government, private volunteer organizations (PVOs), and private sector consulting firms. She lived and worked in Asia for 13 years and has designed, implemented, managed, monitored, and evaluated small enterprise and rural credit programs, as well as worked with self-help housing and school lunch/feeding programs. Most of her experience in the past decade has related to disaster preparedness, mitigation, and crisis management in Africa, both as a PVO staffer and as the head of the Office of U.S. Foreign Disaster Assistance. Borton currently chairs the Management Committee of the Board of the International Rescue Committee, the largest nonsectarian refugee agency in the world.

JENNIFER G. COOKE is deputy director of the CSIS Africa Program. Previously, she worked on the Committee on Human Rights at the National Academy of Sciences and in the academy's Office of News and Public Information. She has also worked on the U.S. House Foreign Affairs Subcommittee on Africa. Cooke, who has lived in Côte d'Ivoire and the Central Africa Republic, earned an M.A. in African studies and international economics from the Johns Hopkins School of Advanced International Studies and a B.A. in government magna cum laude from Harvard University.

JENDAYI E. FRAZER is special assistant to the president and senior director for African affairs at the National Security Council. She was previously assistant professor of public policy at Harvard's Kennedy School of Government and was director of African affairs at the National Security Council in 1999. As a Council on Foreign Relations international affairs fellow, she also spent 1998–1999 as a political-military planner with the Joint Chiefs of Staff. Frazer has been a visiting fellow at Stanford University's Center for International Security and Arms Control, research associate at the Institute for Development Studies at Kenya's University of Nairobi, faculty member of the Graduate School of International Studies, University of Denver, and editor of *Africa Today*. She graduated from Stanford University with a B.A. in political science (honors) and African and African-American studies (distinction), M.A.s in international policy studies and international development education, and a Ph.D. in political science.

JEFFREY I. HERBST is professor of politics and international affairs and chair of the Department of Politics at Princeton University. His primary interests are in the politics of sub-Saharan Africa, the politics of political and economic reform, and the politics of boundaries. He is the author of *States and Power in Africa: Comparative Lessons in Authority and Control* (2000) and several other books and articles. He has also taught at the University of Zimbabwe, the University of Ghana, Legon, the University of Cape Town, and the University of the Western Cape. He is a research associate of the South African Institute of International Affairs. Herbst received a Ph.D. from Yale University.

PETER M. LEWIS is an associate professor at American University's School of International Service in Washington, D.C. He has also served as a fellow at the Woodrow Wilson International Center for Scholars, examining governance and economic change in Indonesia and Nigeria. His research and teaching interests include comparative politics, international political economy, and Third World development. He has taught at Michigan State University and Princeton University and has served at the U.S. embassy in Lagos, Nigeria. Lewis has published articles in *World Politics*, *World Development*, and the *Jour-*

nal of Modern African Studies, in addition to numerous other publications. He has written on the relationship between political and economic reform in Africa, the development of African civil society, and the particular issues of Nigerian political economy.

PRINCETON N. LYMAN is executive director of the Aspen Institute's Global Interdependence Initiative. He is also chairman of the Nigeria Working Group of the Corporate Council on Africa, member of the executive board of the U.S.-South Africa Business Council, and adjunct professor at Georgetown University. Ambassador Lyman's career in government included serving as assistant secretary of state for international organization affairs, U.S. ambassador to South Africa, U.S. ambassador to Nigeria, director of the State Department's Refugee Programs Bureau, and deputy assistant secretary of state for African affairs. Ambassador Lyman is a board member of several philanthropic and civic organizations and author of numerous articles on the United Nations, Africa, foreign policy, and economic development. He received a B.A. from the University of California at Berkeley and a Ph.D. in political science from Harvard University.

TERRENCE P. LYONS is an assistant professor at the Institute for Conflict Analysis and Resolution, George Mason University, Fairfax, Virginia, and a senior associate with the Africa Program at CSIS. He received his Ph.D. from the Johns Hopkins School of Advanced International Studies in 1993. From 1990 until 1998 he served as coordinator of the project on conflict resolution in Africa at the Brookings Institution and conducted research on African security, humanitarian intervention, democratization, and U.S. foreign policy. He has served as a senior researcher and program leader for conflict resolution in peacebuilding at the International Peace Research Institute in Oslo, participated in dispute mediation in Ethiopia, and served as senior program adviser to the Carter Center's project on post-conflict elections in Liberia in 1997. Among his publications are *Voting for Peace: Postconflict Elections in Liberia*, (1999), *Sovereignty as Responsibility: Conflict Management in Africa* (coauthor, 1996), and *Somalia: State Collapse, Multilateral Intervention, and Strategies for Political Reconstruction* (coauthor, 1995).

GWENDOLYN MIKELL is professor of anthropology and director of the African Studies Program in the School of Foreign Service at Georgetown University. She is also president of the African Studies Association and an adjunct senior fellow at the Council of Foreign Relations. Previously, she was a senior fellow at the U.S. Institute of Peace, a member of the Institute for Advanced Study at Princeton, a visiting fellow at the Smithsonian Museum of African Art, and a visiting fellow at the Institute for African Studies at the University of Ghana-Legon and the Institute for Social Research at the University of Natal in Durban, South Africa. She is the author of *Cocoa and Chaos in Ghana* and *African Feminism: The Politics of Survival in Sub-Saharan Africa* and has written articles for numerous journals.

J. STEPHEN MORRISON, director of the CSIS Africa Program, joined CSIS in January 2000 from the Policy Planning Staff at the U.S. Department of State. In 1999, he led the State Department's initiative on illicit diamonds and chaired an interagency review of the U.S. government's crisis humanitarian programs. During 1993–1995, at then USAID administrator J. Brian Atwood's request, Morrison conceptualized and launched USAID's Office of Transition Initiatives, where he served as its first deputy director, created post-conflict field programs in Angola and Bosnia, and worked on other programs in Rwanda and Haiti. From early 1992 until mid-1993 he served as the democracy and governance adviser to the USAID mission and U.S. embassies in Ethiopia and Eritrea. Earlier he was a senior staff member of the U.S. House Foreign Affairs Subcommittee on Africa. An adjunct professor at Johns Hopkins School of Advanced International Studies since 1994, Morrison graduated magna cum laude from Yale College and holds a Ph.D. in political science from the University of Wisconsin.

VICTOR TANNER is an independent consultant and a senior associate of the CSIS Africa Program. He has designed and implemented emergency relief programs in Africa, the Middle East, and the Balkans since 1988 for Médecins Sans Frontières, the International Rescue Committee, ActionAid, Save the Children (UK), UN agencies, and the U.S. Office of Foreign Disaster Assistance (OFDA). He also led a one-year review of the political context in which OFDA implemented programs in the former Yugoslavia (1992–1996). Previously, he was part of USAID's Office of Transition Initiative's Bosnian Federation assessment team and helped establish the International Crisis Group's Dayton-monitoring project in Bosnia in 1996. Tanner has an M.A. in international affairs from Johns Hopkins University School of Advanced International Studies.